GRILLED PIZZA
THE RIGHT WAY

PAGE STREET
PUBLISHING CO.

First published in 2015 by
Page Street Publishing Co.
27 Congress Street, Suite 103
Salem, MA 01970
www.pagestreetpublishing.com

Distributed by Macmillan; sales in Canada by The Canadian Manda Group; distribution in Canada by The Jaguar Book Group.

18 17 16 15   1 2 3 4 5

ISBN-13: 978-1-62414-097-6
ISBN-10: 1-62414-097-1

Library of Congress Control Number: 2014911445

Cover and book design by Page Street Publishing Co.
Photography by Ken Goodman

Printed and bound in China

Page Street is proud to be a member of 1% for the Planet. Members donate one percent of their sales to one or more of the over 1,500 environmental and sustainability charities across the globe who participate in this program.

GRILLED PIZZA
THE RIGHT WAY

THE BEST TECHNIQUE FOR COOKING
INCREDIBLE TASTING PIZZA & FLATBREAD ON YOUR BARBECUE
PERFECTLY CHEWY & CRISPY CRUST EVERY TIME

JOHN DELPHA
WINNER OF TEN JACK DANIEL'S BBQ CHAMPIONSHIP GRILLING AND BBQING AWARDS

PAGE STREET
PUBLISHING CO.

CONTENTS

FRUITS OF THE SEA — 77

GREAT WAYS TO GET YOUR VEGGIES! — 97

THE MASQUERADERS 127

CROSS-BORDER CONTENDERS 147

BRUNCH AND DESSERT FAVORITES 157

FLATBREADS 171

FOREWORD BY KEN ORINGER

Many years ago, John and I worked together at Al Forno, where the grilled pizza was famously invented. I've never seen someone so enthusiastic about food. John will drive four hours out of his way to find something as simple as the best taco or roast beef sandwich. He's obsessed.

That obsession drives his incredible cooking, he respects tradition yet infuses dishes with creativity and flare. That obsession is the inspiration for the amazing food he serves day after day. That obsession is seen in the heap of awards he won for his grilling. And that obsession is right here in this book: a standout collection of recipes built around a unique technique—perfected over the years—for making amazing-tasting pizza on the grill.

These pizzas are like no other. They're easy to make. You can cook them on a gas or charcoal grill. Anyone can do it. They cook fast. They are an open canvas. The results, however, will wow. Pizzas grilled using this technique have a perfectly smoky flavor, and they are crispy and chewy at the same time. You can't get this in a restaurant—at least not in most restaurants. It's really something special.

John is the master of two worlds that normally don't collide. He's a top restaurant chef and outdoor cooking master. The fusion creates something memorable and exceptional you will want to cook and share over and over again.

—Ken Oringer

INTRODUCTION

I was fortunate enough to land my first professional cooking job at Al Forno in Providence, Rhode Island, in 1992. That is where I learned to grill pizza under the direct tutelage of George Germon and Johanne Killeen. George invented grilled pizza in the early 1980's. George wanted to bring the flavors of Italy to the table but didn't have room for a wood-burning oven, so he was inspired to come up with a way to make pizza on the wood-fired open grill at Al Forno. Surprisingly, the dough did not sag through the grill grates and within a few attempts, George had a delicious pizza with all the flavors of authentic Italian pizza and more. The smoke curls around the dough, flavoring the pizza with a haunting light smoky taste. George taught me, and legions of men and women who have trained at Al Forno, how to make those fabulous grilled pizzas. Since then I have gone on to cook in some of the best kitchens in Boston such as Mistral and Clio. I gained my first Executive Chef position at the newly designed and reopened Harvest in Harvard Square; from there I went on to run the kitchen at Gourmet Caterers, which at the time was the largest independent caterer in New England. I moved on to Woodland Golf Club, from there to Executive Chef at Sorellina, which was named one of the best new restaurants by *Esquire* magazine. Then I went on to lead the kitchen at La Campania in Waltham, one of the highest rated Italian restaurants in Boston and the nation. Along the way, I joined the professional competition barbecue cooking team iQue and then opened a restaurant with my wife in Essex, Vermont, called the Belted Cow, which we closed while I was writing this book. During that time I was fortunate enough to have cooked alongside Pitmaster Chris Hart, and in 2009 iQue won the Jack Daniel's World Invitational Barbecue Cooking Championship. I have won the "I Know Jack About Grillin'!" contest twice, as well as the Cook's Choice Category twice and two perfect dessert scores at the Jack Daniel's World Invitational Barbecue Cooking Championship. I have also been lucky enough to win a number of New England Barbecue Society grilling contests. I think I know how to get my grillin' on and wanted to share the knowledge and experience that I have gained with more people.

I am very passionate about open-fire cooking and deeply so of grilled pizza, which is such a unique way to make pizza. The pizzas in this book will have a taste, texture and brightness to them that very few oven-cooked pizzas can replicate. I am a huge fan of wood-oven-cooked pizza, and you probably are too. I want to turn you on to how to properly prepare one of the greatest foods you can easily make for yourself with very few tools, simple ingredients and a grill. Simply put, the right way to grill pizza. When you master the art of grilling pizza, you will amaze and astonish your friends when they first try these pizzas. You instantly have the potential to be the hit at any party with your newly acquired skills.

In this book you will find recipes for savory, sweet and classic pizzas and flatbreads. There are tips to help you succeed. The first pizza in the book, The Anything But Basic Tomato and Cheese Grilled Pizza is a definitive step-by-step instruction that will lead you to grilled-pizza-making nirvana. That is the master recipe that will open the door to endless combinations of toppings for pizza. Once you master how to stretch and grill the crust, feel free to mix up your own ingredients. If I can stress one thing, understanding how to make the crust is the key to the grilled pizza game. Read the first recipe over and over, look at the pictures that will provide you with a visual reference to the words and practice, practice, practice.

Now get started and most of all, have fun!

John Delpha

LEARNING LESSONS, BASIC TECHNIQUES AND EQUIPMENT

Grilling pizza can at first seem daunting. When you read the instructions on The Anything But Basic Tomato and Cheese Grilled Pizza that follows, you will undoubtedly think that it is a lot of work. It really isn't, but it is extremely technique driven. Once you learn the basic technique and continue to advance your skills, you will see that it really isn't that hard to achieve the crispy, smoky crust that is the key to great grilled pizza.

Read this entire chapter, including the tips, before starting. Practice making the shells at least a couple of times before inviting friends over to ensure that you have the technique down. It will get easier, and you will learn how to manage a fire if you are using a charcoal grill. Gas grills are a bit easier.

Equipment: Grill, fuel, grill grate cleaning brush, chimney starter, paper to start the chimney, matches or lighter, tongs (10″ [25.5 cm] suggested), metal pizza peel, half sheet pan or cookie sheet, squeeze bottle, pastry brush, damp towel, dry towel or oven mitt, pizza cutting wheel or knife, workstation adjacent to grill.

Charcoal grill fire management: Light the charcoal in a chimney and keep the coals in the chimney until the coals are all glowing. Dump them on the half of the grill that is opposite your workstation and spread them out evenly. If you can keep the coals contained to one half of the grill you will have a better indirect zone in which to add the ingredients to the pizza. In between making pizzas or stretching out the dough keep the lid on the grill to retain heat and prevent the fire from getting too hot. If needed, you can add coals when your fuel supply has been depleted to less than 50 percent. Keep in mind it will take some time for those coals to ignite and turn a bit ashy before you can use them. You do not want to be cooking a pizza over coals that are on fire.

Gas Grill Management: For 4 burner grills, light the 2 burners on the side of the grill farthest from your workstation on high. Close the grill and let the grates heat about 10 minutes. With 3 burner grills, light the burner farthest from your workstation on high and the middle burner on a medium-low flame. Close the grill and let the grates heat about 10 minutes. Depending on how large your grill is, you may have to turn the middle burner to low.

THE ANYTHING BUT BASIC TOMATO AND CHEESE GRILLED PIZZA

This is the first grilled pizza you should master, as it is the foundation for many other variations. Once you are comfortable making this pizza, it will be much easier to transition to other pizzas with additional ingredients. This pizza relies heavily on superior ingredients and proper technique. When making something as simple as a tomato and cheese pizza, you should work with the best ingredients you can find because lesser quality ingredients will often reveal flaws in imperfect technique or improper preparation. But here is where I contradict myself. I have included store-bought, prepared ingredients in some recipes for the sake of timesaving and convenience.

Take the time to read the recipe instructions and be sure to have all of your ingredients prepared and nearby, placed in containers that are easy to reach into or scoop out of. Remember the Six P's: Prior Planning Prevents Piss-Poor Performance. The level of preparedness is directly proportional to the level of success you will have. Once you get competent with this pizza, be prepared to dazzle your friends with your grill mastery. (For guys, the instant chick magnet thing doesn't hurt either. And any gal who can competently handle a grill is always more attractive.)

➡ YIELDS 3 TO 4 PIZZAS

INGREDIENTS

20 oz (566 g) Pizza Dough (recipe follows) or 1 pound (454 g) store-bought pizza dough

Light cooking oil

Extra virgin olive oil

3 c (420 g) Pizza Cheese Blend (page 20)

3 c (720 ml) Basic Tomato Sauce (page 21)

Sea salt (or kosher salt)

Freshly ground black pepper

6 sprigs flat-leaf parsley picked from stems and sliced thinly

DIRECTIONS

Refer to the equipment list above and set your grilling station up according to the photos on page 16.

Light your grill. Prepare a direct and an indirect zone. The direct cooking side of the grill is the side with the fuel under it. The indirect side of the grill is the side with little or no fuel under it.

Pour about a ¼ cup (60 ml) of cooking oil onto a shallow baking pan or cookie sheet with sides. Make sure your hands are clean and dry. Remove the dough from the refrigerator, and without working it too much, form it into a log about 3 inches (7.62 cm) in diameter on a cutting surface. Cut the dough in half and then each half in half again (approximately 5-ounce [142 g] balls). If you are working with one pound (454 g) of dough, cut it into equal thirds. Pick up each piece of dough and fold the edges underneath and press together to form a ball. Dip the top of the ball in the oil, coat it thoroughly with oil and place on the cookie sheet. Wipe your hands. Repeat with the remaining slices.

The temperature of your work/grilling environment will determine whether you need to refrigerate the balls or leave them out to begin the proofing process. Generally speaking, the dough should be at the proper temperature for stretching in about 10 to 15 minutes in temperate climates.

Place your tomato sauce on a warm spot on the grill just to give it a little heat to take the chill off.

Clean your grill grates with a wire brush after the grill has heated.

Lightly grease an upside-down baking pan or cookie sheet and the palms of your hands. Place one of the balls in the center of the sheet and press down evenly with the palm of your hand. Working with both hands, start in the middle and spread the dough out with your palms while stretching the outer edges with your fingers. You should have an approximately 12 by 8 inch (30 x 20 cm) rectangle if the dough is stretched to a proper thinness.

Lift up the edge farthest from yourself and slide your fingers under the dough. Lift the dough from the cookie sheet. Keep your hands the same distance apart. Move to the direct zone of your grill and place the bottom edge of the dough at the farthest point from you allowing the dough to "catch" on the grill and pull the dough toward you in an even manner until it is completely on the grill. Wipe your hands and grab your tongs. You should be able to see the dough beginning to cook. Gently lift up 1 edge of the dough with the tongs to check for color. When you see some color setting in, lift the dough and give it a quarter turn with the peel. When the dough is sufficiently browned, but not charred, on the bottom, remove it from the direct zone and flip it over onto the indirect zone. The bottom is now the top.

With the dough over the indirect zone, use a squirt bottle to sprinkle some olive oil onto the dough and brush it evenly over the top with the pastry brush. Sprinkle ¾ cup (105 g) of the cheese blend evenly over the dough and then start drizzling the tomato sauce on the dough in a pattern that will ensure you get some sauce in every bite. Do not spread the sauce.

If your grill is too small to create a distinct indirect zone, once you have crisped what will eventually be the top of the pizza, flip the pizza over back onto the direct side of the grill and toast for about 10-15 seconds. Remove the pizza to a metal pizza peel, build the pizza on the peel and then continue with the instructions for crisping the bottom. Toasting the bottom of the pizza before putting it on the peel will make it much easier to slide off the peel. Depending on how hot your fire is, you may need to remove the peel from the grill entirely.

Use the pizza peel to lift the edge of the pizza closest to you and slide the peel under the dough. Move the pizza to the hot zone. Remove the peel. Sprinkle the pizza with the salt, pepper and parsley. Rotate every 15 to 30 seconds to crisp the bottom. Depending on the heat of the grill, after about a minute or so you should see the cheese melting nicely and starting to bubble. Continue rotating the pizza on the peel and back onto the grill to promote an evenly charred and crispy bottom. When the cheese is all melted, the tomato sauce is hot and the bottom is crispy, remove the pizza from the grill with the peel. Drizzle some more olive oil onto the pizza, garnish with the parsley, slice twice lengthwise and three times across and serve. Enjoy. Repeat.

PIZZA DOUGH

➡ YIELDS APPROXIMATELY 10 (5-OUNCE [142 G]) PORTIONS

INGREDIENTS

2¼ c (600 ml) warm water (100°F [38°C])

4 tsp (16 g) yeast

1 tbsp (12 g) sugar

2 tbsp (30 ml) extra virgin olive oil

5 c (640 g) all purpose flour

½ c (64 g) semolina

1 tbsp (12 g) salt

DIRECTIONS

Place water, yeast and sugar in the bowl of a stand mixer. Let sit for 5 minutes until yeast is activated (bubbly). Add oil, then add dry ingredients. Place a dough hook on the mixer and turn to medium low. Mix for approximately 5 minutes until a smooth ball appears. Turn the mixer to medium high and knead for approximately 2 minutes until the ball obtains a light shine. The dough can be put in a bag and refrigerated for use within the next 3 days or frozen for up to a month.

PIZZA CHEESE BLEND

This is a simple base of cheese for the majority of pizzas in the book. Feel free to experiment with your own favorites.

➡ YIELDS 2 POUNDS (454 G)

INGREDIENTS

1 lb (454 g) Cheddar cheese, shredded

½ lb (227 g) Parmesan cheese, grated

½ lb (227 g) Pecorino Romano cheese, grated

DIRECTIONS

Add all of the cheeses to a large bowl and stir to combine. Keep in a sealed container in the refrigerator until ready to use.

BASIC TOMATO SAUCE

I prefer to use whole peeled tomatoes in heavy purée for the sauce. My favorite brands of late are Nina, Redpack and Teresa. The sauce is uncooked to try to retain a certain lightness and just a small addition of garlic and salt is all you need.

➜ YIELDS 2³/₄ CUPS (700 ML)

INGREDIENTS

2 cloves garlic, peeled and finely minced

1 tbsp (15 ml) extra virgin olive oil

1 (28-oz [794 g]) can whole, peeled tomatoes in heavy purée

1 tsp (6 g) kosher salt

DIRECTIONS

Sauté the garlic in olive oil over medium heat until the garlic is translucent, about 1 to 2 minutes. Remove from the heat.

Empty the tomatoes into a small mixing bowl and crush the tomatoes into small chunks by hand. Add the garlic, oil and the salt and stir to combine. Reserve until needed.

SOME TIPS

Practice alone first.

Stretch the dough as thin as you can all the way to the edges. The oiliness and thinness of the dough are key to creating a crispy crust.

Shape the pizza to fit into the boundaries of your cooking zones.

The pizza dough ball should be well-oiled before stretching. If the dough gets crusty or dry it is because it isn't oily enough.

Make sure that your dough is a temperature that will allow stretching without much difficulty (this is called proofing). Underproofed dough will be rubbery and difficult to stretch. Give it a little more time to warm up.

Overproofed dough is easy to stretch, but rips easily, which could cause you to put holes in the dough as you stretch. Put the dough back in the refrigerator to keep it chilled until just before using it.

Make sure everything you need including tools, pizza ingredients and service ware are all within reach before you begin.

Do not plop or drop the dough onto the grill. This will cause the dough to droop between the grates.

This pizza is not like other pizzas you may have made. Do not stretch the dough on a floured surface and do not create a lip around the edge of the crust.

Frozen dough will need a few days in the fridge to thaw.

Find freshly prepared dough in the deli case at many grocery stores. Manufactured dough in tubes may or may not yield a good result.

THE CLASSICS

Classics remain because they are mainstays of society. I can't think of any Neapolitan pizzeria that doesn't serve a Pizza Margherita. Some of the pizzas in this chapter may not be typical classics, but they are classics to me because I have been eating them for a long time. The first bite of a pizza with peppers agro dolce and prosciutto instantly entered my hall of fame—try it, I hope you will agree. The Tribute to Providence Pizza is a classic for me because it triggers wonderful childhood pizza memories. It is a pizza I still yearn for today, so I have done my best to transfer those flavors to a grilled pizza. Summer corn, tomato and mozzarella is certainly a late August classic flavor combination where I grew up, and the ingredients work so perfectly on a pizza. Try them all. I am sure they won't disappoint. Cheers to the classics, here and now, those gone by and yours and mine!

PIZZA MARGHERITA

This is the pizza by which I evaluate almost every Neapolitan-style pizzeria. If they can make a really good Pizza Margherita, then I am willing to try some of their other creations. Simplicity shines through here. I know traditionally it is just tomato sauce, Mozzarella and basil, but I like to add the Pizza Cheese Blend for a little additional flavor. Feel free to leave it out if you yearn for traditionalism.

➡ YIELDS I PIZZA

INGREDIENTS

5 oz (142 g) oiled Pizza Dough ball (page 17)

¾ c (105 g) Pizza Cheese Blend (page 20)

¾ c (180 ml) Basic Tomato Sauce (page 21)

2 oz (56 g) fresh Mozzarella, thinly sliced

Extra virgin olive oil

6 fresh basil leaves, torn into pieces

DIRECTIONS

Lightly grease a metal work surface and the palms of your hands. Place the dough ball in the center of the surface and press down evenly with the palm of your hand. Working with both hands, start in the middle and spread the dough out with your palms while stretching the outer edges with your fingers. You should have an approximately 12 by 8 inch (30 x 20 cm) rectangle.

Lift up the edge farthest from yourself and slide your fingers under the dough. Move to the direct zone of your grill and place the bottom edge of the dough at the farthest point from you and pull the dough toward you to place on grill. Gently lift up 1 edge of the dough with the tongs to check for color. When you see some color setting in, lift the dough and give it a quarter turn with the peel. When the dough is sufficiently browned on the bottom, but not charred, remove it from the direct zone and flip it over onto the indirect zone. The bottom is now the top.

When you turn over the pizza onto the indirect side of the grill, brush with olive oil, sprinkle on the cheese blend, place slices of Mozzarella all around the pizza and spoon the sauce in dollops all over, remembering not to spread the sauce out. Move the pizza to the direct side of the grill and rotate every 15 to 30 seconds to crisp the bottom. When the bottom is crispy and the cheese is melted, remove from the grill, drizzle with olive oil and scatter the basil all over, slice and serve.

ROASTED PEPPERS AGRO DOLCE, PROSCIUTTO AND PARMIGIANO PIZZA

This pizza is an absolute fan favorite. Based upon the Anything But Basic Pizza, we continue with the simplicity and add a couple of knockout punches. We start by charring sweet red peppers and marinating them Agro Dolce style, which is Italian for sweet and sour. Then we add the silky texture and salty flavor of thinly sliced Italian prosciutto, finished with an umami kick from the king of all cheeses, shaved Parmigiano. You are taking your friends on a trip down taste sensory lane. I would have said to flavortown, but I think someone has coined that phrase already, and I certainly don't need any copyright infringements in my first book. Enjoy this with a nice cold glass of crisp Falanghina.

➡ YIELDS 1 PIZZA

INGREDIENTS

5 oz (142 g) oiled Pizza Dough ball (page 17)

Extra virgin olive oil

¾ c (105 g) Pizza Cheese Blend (page 20)

¾ c (180 ml) Basic Tomato Sauce (page 21)

⅓ c (30 g) Peppers Agro Dolce (page 28)

Freshly ground black pepper

Large pinch of thinly sliced flat-leaf parsley

5-6 thinly sliced pieces of prosciutto

2 tbsp (15 g) shaved Parmigiano

DIRECTIONS

Lightly grease a metal work surface and the palms of your hands. Place the dough ball in the center of the surface and press down evenly with the palm of your hand. Working with both hands, start in the middle and spread the dough out with your palms while stretching the outer edges with your fingers. You should have an approximately 12 by 8 inch (30 x 20 cm) rectangle.

Lift up the edge farthest from yourself and slide your fingers under the dough. Move to the direct zone of your grill and place the bottom edge of the dough at the farthest point from you and pull the dough toward you to place on grill. Gently lift up 1 edge of the dough with the tongs to check for color. When you see some color setting in, lift the dough and give it a quarter turn with the peel. When the dough is sufficiently browned on the bottom, but not charred, remove it from the direct zone and flip it over onto the indirect zone. The bottom is now the top.

Drizzle with olive oil and brush the crust evenly. Sprinkle the cheese all around the crust and add dollops of tomato sauce. After adding the tomato sauce add about 9 strips of roasted peppers agro dolce and some of the raisins in the marinade around the pizza (be sure to leave the raw garlic behind in the marinade and not on the pizza). Sprinkle pepper and parsley around the pizza and cook to desired doneness. Working quickly, remove the pizza from the heat and top with the prosciutto and shaved Parmigiano. Drizzle again with olive oil, slice and serve.

PEPPERS AGRO DOLCE

Agro dolce is Italian for "sweet and sour." These peppers are excellent additions to antipasto platters, grilled pizza, sandwiches, salads and grilled meats. Make more than what you need so you can keep some on hand. Charring the peppers gives them a nice smokiness that works well with the sweetness of the raisins and the tartness of the balsamic. They will keep for a month in the refrigerator.

➡ YIELDS 1 CUP (90 G)

INGREDIENTS

2 tbsp (20 g) each dark raisins and golden raisins

2 red bell peppers

2 cloves garlic, smashed

¼ c (60 ml) balsamic vinegar

2 tbsp (30 ml) extra virgin olive oil

Salt

Freshly ground black pepper

DIRECTIONS

If you have an open-flame gas burner stove you can char the peppers on that. If not you can use the grill or broiler.

Soak the raisins in hot water to plump and rehydrate. Char the peppers evenly over a very hot fire all the way around. All the skin should be blistered. Remove the peppers and place in a bowl and cover with plastic wrap. Let sit for about 10 minutes. When peppers are cool enough to handle but not completely cold, rub the skins off the peppers with your hands or a kitchen towel. Tear open the peppers over a bowl to reserve the juices inside. Remove the stem and seeds and discard. Slice the peppers lengthwise into ⅛ to ¼ inch (3 to 6 mm) pieces. Return to the bowl with whatever juices may have leaked out when you tore them open. Drain the raisins from the water and add to the peppers. Add the remaining ingredients and season to taste. Stir and then marinate for at least an hour at room temperature. Cover and refrigerate.

SAUSAGE, TOMATO AND MUSHROOM PIZZA

Here is another easy-to-make variation of the Anything But Basic Pizza. Don't limit yourself only to the suggestions in this book. Be creative and if you see something in your pantry or fridge you think would work on a grilled pizza, go ahead and try it.

 YIELDS I PIZZA

INGREDIENTS

8 oz (227 g) cooked sweet Italian sausages, peeled from their skins

5 oz (142 g) oiled Pizza Dough ball (page 17)

Extra virgin olive oil

¾ c (105 g) Pizza Cheese Blend (page 20)

¼ c (35 g) Cooked Cremini Mushrooms (page 31)

¾ c (180 ml) Basic Tomato Sauce (page 21)

Thinly sliced flat-leaf parsley for garnish

DIRECTIONS

Cut the sausages into large pieces and place in the bowl of a food processor and pulse until you get a fine crumble (about the size of small peas).

Lightly grease a metal work surface and the palms of your hands. Place the dough ball in the center of the surface and press down evenly with the palm of your hand. Working with both hands, start in the middle and spread the dough out with your palms while stretching the outer edges with your fingers. You should have an approximately 12 by 8 inch (30 x 20 cm) rectangle.

Lift up the edge farthest from yourself and slide your fingers under the dough. Move to the direct zone of your grill and place the bottom edge of the dough at the farthest point from you and pull the dough toward you to place on grill. Gently lift up 1 edge of the dough with the tongs to check for color. When you see some color setting in, lift the dough and give it a quarter turn with the peel. When the dough is sufficiently browned on the bottom, but not charred, remove it from the direct zone and flip it over onto the indirect zone. The bottom is now the top.

Drizzle with olive oil and brush the crust evenly. Sprinkle the cheese all over and add the sausage and mushrooms. Spoon dollops of the tomato sauce all around the pizza. Move the pizza to the direct side of the grill and rotate every 15 to 30 seconds to crisp the bottom. When the bottom is crispy remove the pizza from the grill, drizzle with olive oil, add the parsley, slice and serve.

COOKED CREMINI MUSHROOMS

→ YIELDS ½ CUP (70 G)

INGREDIENTS

1 tbsp (15 ml) extra virgin olive oil

1 clove garlic, chopped

4 oz (113 g) medium button mushrooms, sliced

Salt

Freshly ground pepper

DIRECTIONS

Heat the oil in a medium-size skillet, add the garlic and cook until translucent, add the mushrooms and cook stirring now and again until all the liquid is evaporated. Season with salt and pepper. Remove from the pan and cool in the refrigerator until needed.

SUMMER TOMATO, CORN AND MOZZARELLA PIZZA

Nothing quite says summer more than warm vine-ripened local tomatoes and fresh corn. Here in New England we are blessed with farmers who provide us with some of the nicest produce. While I do enjoy raw corn right off the cob, I think toasting it over the coals provides an extra layer of flavor.

➡ YIELDS I PIZZA

INGREDIENTS

1 ear sweet corn, shucked (preferably Silver Queen or Butter & Sugar)

Extra virgin olive oil

Salt

Pepper

1 medium to large ripe tomato, sliced about a ¼-inch (6 mm) thick

5 oz (142 g) oiled Pizza Dough ball (page 17)

½ c (70 g) Pizza Cheese Blend (page 20)

3 oz (85 g) fresh Mozzarella, thinly sliced

6 basil leaves torn into quarters

One small pinch thinly sliced flat-leaf parsley

DIRECTIONS

Toast the corn briefly on the grill to activate the sugars. You don't want the kernels to turn black, but light shades of brown will be just fine. Slice the kernels from the cob and toss in a bowl with olive oil, salt, pepper and parsley.

Lightly season the tomato slices with olive oil, salt and pepper.

Clean the grill.

Lightly grease a metal work surface and the palms of your hands. Place the dough ball in the center of the surface and press down evenly with the palm of your hand. Working with both hands, start in the middle and spread the dough out with your palms while stretching the outer edges with your fingers. You should have an approximately 12 by 8 inch (30 x 20 cm) rectangle.

Lift up the edge farthest from yourself and slide your fingers under the dough. Move to the direct zone of your grill and place the bottom edge of the dough at the farthest point from you and pull the dough toward you to place on grill. Gently lift up 1 edge of the dough with the tongs to check for color. When you see some color setting in, lift the dough and give it a quarter turn with the peel. When the dough is sufficiently browned on the bottom, but not charred, remove it from the direct zone and flip it over onto the indirect zone. The bottom is now the top.

Drizzle with olive oil and brush the crust evenly. Sprinkle on the cheese blend evenly and distribute the Mozzarella all around the crust. Return to the indirect side and add the tomatoes, leaving some spaces between the slices. Sprinkle corn all around. Move the crust back to the direct side and rotate every 15 to 30 seconds and crisp up to desired doneness. Drizzle some olive oil all around and remove from the grill. Spread the torn basil leaves and parsley all around, slice and serve.

Pretty damn good, right? Thank a farmer and Mother Nature. Maybe a little pat on the back for your pizza grilling skills. Extra kudos if you grew the tomatoes and corn too.

PIZZA AMATRICIANA

All'Amatriciana is a classic pasta sauce in Roman cookery. Pancetta is usually called for in the recipe in Italy, but here I like to use good old American smoked bacon. By all means substitute the pancetta if you prefer.

➡ YIELDS 1 PIZZA

INGREDIENTS

5 oz (142 g) oiled Pizza Dough ball (page 17)

Extra virgin olive oil

1 c (140 g) Pizza Cheese Blend (page 20)

1 c (180 ml) Amatriciana Sauce (page 35)

¼ c (35 g) grated Pecorino Romano

2 large pinches of sliced flat-leaf parsley

DIRECTIONS

Lightly grease a metal work surface and the palms of your hands. Place the dough ball in the center of the surface and press down evenly with the palm of your hand. Working with both hands, start in the middle and spread the dough out with your palms while stretching the outer edges with your fingers. You should have an approximately 12 by 8 inch (30 x 20 cm) rectangle.

Lift up the edge farthest from yourself and slide your fingers under the dough. Move to the direct zone of your grill and place the bottom edge of the dough at the farthest point from you and pull the dough toward you to place on grill. Gently lift up 1 edge of the dough with the tongs to check for color. When you see some color setting in, lift the dough and give it a quarter turn with the peel. When the dough is sufficiently browned on the bottom, but not charred, remove it from the direct zone and flip it over onto the indirect zone. The bottom is now the top.

Drizzle with olive oil and brush the crust evenly. Sprinkle on the cheese blend and place dollops of the sauce all around the pizza giving good coverage but leaving minor gaps between dollops. Return the pizza to the direct side of the grill and rotate every 15 to 30 seconds until the bottom is crispy, the cheese bubbles and the sauce is hot. Remove the pizza, sprinkle the Romano and parsley all around, slice and serve.

AMATRICIANA SAUCE

→ YIELDS 3½ CUPS (840 ML)

INGREDIENTS

2 tbsp (30 ml) extra virgin olive oil

3 garlic cloves, smashed and chopped

1½ tsp (7.5 g) red chili flakes, more if you like it spicier

6 slices of smoked bacon cut into ½ inch (13 mm) pieces

½ small red onion, sliced thinly against the grain then cut in half again

½ c (120 ml) dry white wine

3 c (720 ml) Basic Tomato Sauce (page 21)

DIRECTIONS

Heat the olive oil, garlic, chili flakes, bacon and onion in a saucepan on medium high heat.

Cook until the onions are soft, the garlic is lightly toasted and the bacon is rendered. The chili flakes will give the oil a nice red hue. Add the white wine and reduce by half. Add the tomato sauce, bring to a boil, reduce to a simmer and cook for 5 to 7 minutes. Remove from the pan and reserve. This makes more than you need for one pizza, but as I mentioned earlier, it is a classic pasta sauce in Italy and it never hurts to have some of it on hand. It will store well in the refrigerator for a week or for a couple of months in the freezer.

QUATTRO STAGIONE PIZZA

The **Quattro Stagione Pizza** uses four different ingredients to represent the four seasons—artichokes for spring, olives for summer, mushrooms for fall and prosciutto for winter. I suggest sharing this pizza with one other person, slicing the pizza along the seasonal lines and then slicing each season in half so you each get a piece of a season. Of course if you want to make this pizza all for yourself then go for it.

 YIELDS 1 PIZZA

INGREDIENTS

5 oz (142 g) oiled Pizza Dough ball (page 17)

Extra virgin olive oil

¾ c (105 g) Pizza Cheese Blend (page 20)

¾ c (180 ml) Basic Tomato Sauce (page 21)

¼ c (35 g) marinated artichoke hearts

2 tbsp (17 g) pitted, chopped black olives such as Gaeta

¼ c (35 g) Cooked Cremini Mushrooms (page 31)

2-3 thin slices of prosciutto

Thinly sliced flat-leaf parsley, for garnish

DIRECTIONS

Lightly grease a metal work surface and the palms of your hands. Place the dough ball in the center of the surface and press down evenly with the palm of your hand. Working with both hands, start in the middle and spread the dough out with your palms while stretching the outer edges with your fingers. You should have an approximately 12 by 8 inch (30 x 20 cm) rectangle.

Lift up the edge farthest from yourself and slide your fingers under the dough. Move to the direct zone of your grill and place the bottom edge of the dough at the farthest point from you and pull the dough toward you to place on grill. Gently lift up 1 edge of the dough with the tongs to check for color. When you see some color setting in, lift the dough and give it a quarter turn with the peel. When the dough is sufficiently browned on the bottom, but not charred, remove it from the direct zone and flip it over onto the indirect zone. The bottom is now the top.

Drizzle with olive oil and brush the crust. Sprinkle the cheese over the crust evenly. Spoon dollops of the tomato sauce all around the pizza. Visualize the pizza in 4 quadrants, add the artichokes in the top left quadrant, the olives to the top right quadrant, mushrooms to the bottom right quadrant and reserve the bottom left quadrant for the prosciutto after you remove the pizza from the grill. Move the pizza to the direct side of the grill and rotate every 15 to 30 seconds until the pizza is crispy. When the bottom is crispy, remove the pizza from the grill, sprinkle with parsley, place the prosciutto in the bottom left quadrant, drizzle with olive oil, slice as suggested above and serve.

GRILLED PIZZA BOLOGNESE

Bolognese sauce, known in Italian as *ragú alla Bolognese*, is a meat-based sauce that originated in Bologna, Italy. The sauce recipe here originated with my good friends Dean and Kate about 9 years ago. This is a lighter version of the original but no less delicious. I put the veal ragú on the menu at La Campania, and within 2 days the servers were calling it "crack." In food land, that's a high honor. Other than the chicken wing rub I use, the veal ragú was always the recipe people would ask if they could have. They would be shocked when I would hand them a printed copy and wonder why I would give up a house secret like that. I did it to share and hoped they would make the recipe for friends and family, which is how the recipe originated. As for the wing rub, I would sell them as much of it as they wanted. Just don't ask for the recipe—ya gotta draw the line sometimes. Try it with a Bonarda or a chilled Lambrusco.

 YIELDS | PIZZA

INGREDIENTS

1¼ c (360 ml) Veal Ragú (page 39)

5 oz (142 g) oiled Pizza Dough ball (page 17)

Extra virgin olive oil

¾ c (105 ml) Pizza Cheese Blend (page 20)

2 tbsp (17 g) grated Parmesan

Thinly sliced flat-leaf parsley, for garnish

DIRECTIONS

In a small saucepan heat the ragú up on a warm part of the grill.

Lightly grease a metal work surface and the palms of your hands. Place the dough ball in the center of the surface and press down evenly with the palm of your hand. Working with both hands, start in the middle and spread the dough out with your palms while stretching the outer edges with your fingers. You should have an approximately 12 by 8 inch (30 x 20 cm) rectangle.

Lift up the edge farthest from yourself and slide your fingers under the dough. Move to the direct zone of your grill and place the bottom edge of the dough at the farthest point from you and pull the dough toward you to place on grill. Gently lift up 1 edge of the dough with the tongs to check for color. When you see some color setting in, lift the dough and give it a quarter turn with the peel. When the dough is sufficiently browned on the bottom, but not charred, remove it from the direct zone and flip it over onto the indirect zone. The bottom is now the top.

Drizzle with olive oil and brush the crust evenly. Spread the cheese all over the crust and spoon the sauce all over the pizza trying to cover the whole area. Move the pizza to the hot side of the grill and rotate every 15 to 30 seconds to crisp the bottom. When the bottom is crispy, remove the pizza, sprinkle with the Parmesan and parsley, slice and serve.

VEAL RAGÚ

INGREDIENTS

¼ c (60 ml) extra virgin olive oil

5 cloves garlic, chopped

1 medium yellow onion, diced fine

4 oz (113 g) pancetta, chopped fine

2½ lb (1.1 kg) ground veal (preferably organic)

1 c (240 ml) white wine

2 c (480 ml) whole peeled tomatoes in heavy purée, puréed in a blender

2 tbsp (3 g) fresh rosemary leaves, chopped fine

¼ c (15 g) flat-leaf parsley, thinly sliced

½ c (120 ml) heavy cream

Salt

Freshly ground black pepper

1 tbsp (14 g) unsalted butter

½ c (70 g) grated Parmesan cheese

DIRECTIONS

Heat oil in large saucepan over medium heat.

Add the garlic, onion and pancetta and cook until soft and translucent (no color).

Add veal and cook until moisture is evaporated (remove fat).

Add the wine, tomatoes and 1 tablespoon (1.5 g) of rosemary. Simmer for 1 hour.

When finished, stir in additional rosemary, parsley and cream. Season with salt and pepper.

Cool and store.

When reheating, add butter and Parmesan cheese.

THE SALTIMBOCCA GRILLED PIZZA

One of my favorite dishes is Chicken or Veal Saltimbocca with mushrooms that have been glazed in Marsala wine. It's actually on my death row list of things to eat. Marsala has a sweet, full and warm flavor to it that I think goes nicely with the earthiness of the mushrooms. *Saltimbocca* in Italian literally means "jump in the mouth." Open wide!

➡ YIELDS 1 PIZZA

INGREDIENTS

1 small boneless skinless chicken breast (about 4 oz [113 g])

Extra virgin olive oil

Salt

Freshly ground black pepper

5 oz (142 g) oiled Pizza Dough ball (page 17)

¾ c (105 g) Pizza Cheese Blend (page 20)

3–4 medium-size fresh sage leaves, torn into small pieces

⅓ c (43 g) Cooked Marsala Mushrooms (page 41)

4–5 pieces thinly sliced prosciutto

Thinly sliced chives, for garnish

DIRECTIONS

Rub the chicken lightly with oil and season with salt and pepper. Place the chicken over a medium-heat fire on the grill. Cook the chicken, turning several times until an instant-read thermometer placed in the thickest part of the breast registers 165°F (74°C). Remove the chicken from the grill and let rest. When cool enough to handle, shred the chicken in lengthwise strips and reserve.

Clean the grill.

Lightly grease a metal work surface and the palms of your hands. Place the dough ball in the center of the surface and press down evenly with the palm of your hand. Working with both hands, start in the middle and spread the dough out with your palms while stretching the outer edges with your fingers. You should have an approximately 12 by 8 inch (30 x 20 cm) rectangle.

Lift up the edge farthest from yourself and slide your fingers under the dough. Move to the direct zone of your grill and place the bottom edge of the dough at the farthest point from you and pull the dough toward you to place on grill. Gently lift up 1 edge of the dough with the tongs to check for color. When you see some color setting in, lift the dough and give it a quarter turn with the peel. When the dough is sufficiently browned on the bottom, but not charred, remove it from the direct zone and flip it over onto the indirect zone. The bottom is now the top.

Drizzle with olive oil and brush the crust evenly. Sprinkle the cheese and add the chicken and sage leaves. Spoon the mushrooms all over and drizzle any remaining sauce from the bowl onto the pizza. Close the lid of the grill to heat the toppings a bit. Move the pizza to the hot side of the grill and rotate every 15 to 30 seconds to crisp the bottom. When the bottom is crispy, remove from the grill, drizzle with olive oil, place the prosciutto slices, sprinkle with chives, slice and serve.

COOKED MARSALA MUSHROOMS

→ YIELDS ½ CUP (70 G)

INGREDIENTS

1 tbsp (15 ml) extra virgin olive oil
2 tbsp (28 g) unsalted butter
4 oz (113 g) button mushrooms, sliced
2 tbsp (30 ml) sweet Marsala wine
2 tbsp (30 ml) dry Marsala wine
Salt
Freshly ground black pepper

DIRECTIONS

Heat the oil and a ½ tablespoon (7 g) of butter in a skillet over medium heat. When the butter begins to sizzle, add the mushrooms and cook until all the liquid has evaporated. Add both types of Marsala and reduce ¾, add the remaining butter, melt the butter, stir to incorporate and remove from the heat. Transfer to a bowl, season with salt and pepper and reserve.

GRILLED PORK AND VINEGAR PEPPERS PIZZA

Cheese-filled grilled pork chops with vinegar peppers has been a longtime favorite meal for me. It's an old-school Italian classic that just keeps me coming back for more. On Memorial Day weekend I made them for dinner on Saturday night. When I woke up Sunday I just knew I had to include a grilled pizza version. Here's a recipe for vinegar peppers, but I highly encourage you to try the Pastene brand version as I'm a huge fan, but by all means feel free to make your own. I like to drink a young Chianti Classico with this.

 YIELDS 1 PIZZA

INGREDIENTS

6 oz (170 g) pork tenderloin, butt section, trimmed of all sinew

Salt

Freshly ground black pepper

1 tbsp (14 g) unsalted butter

1 small clove garlic, thinly sliced

⅓ c (43 g) sliced Vinegar Peppers (¼ x 1 inch [6 x 25 mm] slices) (page 44)

1 tbsp (15 ml) vinegar pepper juice

5 oz (142 g) oiled Pizza Dough ball (page 17)

2 c (280 g) shredded Jarlsberg cheese (or Swiss)

Extra virgin olive oil

Thinly sliced flat-leaf parsley, for garnish

DIRECTIONS

Season the pork with salt and freshly ground black pepper. Place over a medium-heat fire and cook turning constantly to medium rare to medium about 8 minutes (130°F [54°C] on an instant-read thermometer). Remove from the grill and let rest. Just before making the pizza, slice the tenderloin diagonally across the grain in ¼ inch (6 mm) slices (about 12 slices).

Clean the grill.

Heat butter in a skillet over medium heat, add the garlic and cook until translucent about 1 to 2 minutes, add the peppers and the pepper juice and reduce the liquid by half, reserve and keep warm.

Lightly grease a metal work surface and the palms of your hands. Place the dough ball in the center of the surface and press down evenly with the palm of your hand. Working with both hands, start in the middle and spread the dough out with your palms while stretching the outer edges with your fingers. You should have an approximately 12 by 8 inch (30 x 20 cm) rectangle.

Lift up the edge farthest from yourself and slide your fingers under the dough. Move to the direct zone of your grill and place the bottom edge of the dough at the farthest point from you and pull the dough toward you to place on grill. Gently lift up 1 edge of the dough with the tongs to check for color. When you see some color setting in, lift the dough and give it a quarter turn with the peel. When the dough is sufficiently browned on the bottom, but not charred, remove it from the direct zone and flip it over onto the indirect zone. The bottom is now the top.

Drizzle with olive oil and brush the crust evenly. Spread 1 cup (140 g) of the Jarlsberg cheese all around the crust, arrange the pork slices on the pizza, and add the sliced vinegar peppers, sprinkle the remaining cheese around trying to hit each piece of pork with a little. Close the lid of the grill for 1 minute to help warm the pork. Move the pizza to the direct side of the grill and rotate every 15 to 30 seconds to crisp the bottom. When the bottom is crispy drizzle the butter/garlic/vinegar juice all over the pizza, garnish with the parsley, slice and serve.

VINEGAR PEPPERS

INGREDIENTS

¾ c (180 ml) white vinegar

¼ c (60 ml) red wine vinegar

⅓ c (79 ml) water

1½ tsp (7.5 g) red pepper flakes

4 red and yellow bell peppers, julienned

DIRECTIONS

Bring the vinegar, water and pepper flakes to a boil over medium heat. Pour the liquid over the peppers and let stand at least 15 minutes.

Cool, cover and refrigerate. Will last for up to a month in the fridge.

THE CLASSIC PEPPERONI PIZZA

Pepperoni, also known as pepperoni sausage, is an American cured salami made from pork and beef. Pepperoni is characteristically soft, slightly smoky and dark red in color. Chances are you have had a pepperoni pizza. For the grilled version we sear the pepperoni lightly on the grill to give it a little crisping and intensify the flavor a bit. If you can't find the larger diameter sandwich pepperoni, the smaller version is fine.

Have an ice-cold beer with this pizza!

 YIELDS | PIZZA

INGREDIENTS

9 thin slices of the larger diameter sandwich pepperoni

5 oz (142 g) oiled Pizza Dough ball (page 17)

Extra virgin olive oil

¾ c (105 g) Pizza Cheese Blend (page 20)

¾ c (180 ml) Basic Tomato Sauce (page 21)

Thinly sliced flat-leaf parsley, for garnish

DIRECTIONS

Place the pepperoni slices over the direct portion of the grill and let crisp up slightly turning once, about 30 seconds per side, remove and reserve.

Clean the grill.

Lightly grease a metal work surface and the palms of your hands. Place the dough ball in the center of the surface and press down evenly with the palm of your hand. Working with both hands, start in the middle and spread the dough out with your palms while stretching the outer edges with your fingers. You should have an approximately 12 by 8 inch (30 x 20 cm) rectangle.

Lift up the edge farthest from yourself and slide your fingers under the dough. Move to the direct zone of your grill and place the bottom edge of the dough at the farthest point from you and pull the dough toward you to place on grill. Gently lift up 1 edge of the dough with the tongs to check for color. When you see some color setting in, lift the dough and give it a quarter turn with the peel. When the dough is sufficiently browned on the bottom, but not charred, remove it from the direct zone and flip it over onto the indirect zone. The bottom is now the top.

When you turn over the crust onto the indirect side of the grill, drizzle with olive oil and brush the crust evenly. Sprinkle the cheese all over, place the slices of pepperoni on the pizza and spoon dollops of tomato sauce all around, remembering not to spread the sauce out. Move the pizza to the direct side of the grill and rotate every 15 to 30 seconds to crisp the bottom. When the bottom is crispy and the toppings hot, remove the pizza, drizzle with oil, sprinkle on the parsley, slice and serve.

TRIBUTE TO PROVIDENCE PIZZA

When I was growing up in Providence one of my favorite treats was the Everything But Anchovy Pizza from Caserta Pizzeria on Federal Hill. It's a Sicilian-style pizza, not too thick, not too thin, best when ordered well done so the crust is crispy. It's topped with a zesty tomato sauce, whole-milk Mozzarella, pepperoni, mushrooms and black olives. Here is the grilled version.

 YIELDS I PIZZA

INGREDIENTS

2 tbsp (30 ml) extra virgin olive oil, plus more for the pizza

2 cloves of garlic, finely minced

1½ c (360 ml) Basic Tomato Sauce (page 21)

1 tsp (4 g) granulated sugar

½ c (30 g) sliced button mushrooms

Salt

Freshly ground black pepper

6–7 thin slices of the larger diameter sandwich pepperoni (smaller pepperoni is fine, but you will need more slices)

5 oz (142 g) oiled Pizza Dough ball (page 17)

1 c (140 g) shredded whole-milk Mozzarella

¼ c (35 g) chopped black olives

DIRECTIONS

Place 1 tablespoon (15 ml) of olive oil in a small saucepan and heat slowly, add the garlic and cook until translucent. Add the tomato sauce and continue to cook over low heat until the sauce is reduced and very thick, around 30 minutes. You are trying to eliminate extra liquid and concentrate the tomatoes. Remove from the heat and add the teaspoon (4 g) of sugar, season with salt and pepper. You should have about a cup of sauce when finished.

Heat a medium skillet over medium heat, add 1 tablespoon (15 ml) olive oil then add the mushrooms. Cook until all of the liquid has evaporated and the mushrooms are lightly browned, about 5 minutes. Season with salt and pepper.

Lightly crisp the pepperoni on the grill and then clean the grill.

Lightly grease a metal work surface and the palms of your hands. Place the dough ball in the center of the surface and press down evenly with the palm of your hand. Working with both hands, start in the middle and spread the dough out with your palms while stretching the outer edges with your fingers. You should have an approximately 12 by 8 inch (30 x 20 cm) rectangle.

Lift up the edge farthest from yourself and slide your fingers under the dough. Move to the direct zone of your grill and place the bottom edge of the dough at the farthest point from you and pull the dough toward you to place on grill. Gently lift up 1 edge of the dough with the tongs to check for color. When you see some color setting in, lift the dough and give it a quarter turn with the peel. When the dough is sufficiently browned on the bottom, but not charred, remove it from the direct zone and flip it over onto the indirect zone. The bottom is now the top.

Drizzle with olive oil and brush the crust evenly. Add the tomato sauce and spread all over the crust with the back of a spoon. Sprinkle the cheese all over. Add the mushrooms and olives. Arrange the pepperoni slices around the pizza and close the lid of the grill to help get the cheese melted and the toppings hot for 1–2 minutes. It may take a little longer; just be sure to check on the pizza to make sure the bottom doesn't get burned. If the bottom hasn't crisped sufficiently, move the pizza to the direct side of the grill and rotate every 15 to 30 seconds. When the bottom is crispy remove from the grill, slice and serve.

MEAT PIZZAS

Beef, pork (in many different ways), duck and lamb all find their way onto these pizzas. Savory, big, bold flavors all await you ahead in this chapter. Alpine flavors in the Tartiflette and Bresaola, Raclette and Cornichon pizzas will all leave you fully sated. The sweet, sour-salty magic of the award-winning Duck Confit, Black Fig, Blue Cheese and Balsamic Pizza will have you making extras for your ride to work. The Shaved Brussels Sprouts, Bacon, Pecorino and Mozzarella will leave you with a very different impression of what you may have thought brussels sprouts were. Try them all and make up some of your very own. Be adventurous, if anything, it is fun to try.

TARTIFLETTE PIZZA

Tartiflette is a French dish usually found in the Savoie and Haute Savoie region of France. It is a simple dish of potatoes, bacon, onions and Reblochon cheese. The first time I had it was in a small restaurant in the city of Chambery. I had spent the day hiking in the nearby Alps and by the end of the day was famished. It's a good thing, because Tartiflette is not a light dish nor for the faint of heart. Reblochon is not available in the United States because of the absurd rules about raw milk. A good substitute is Préférés de nos Montagnes, which should be available in cheese shops. Tartiflette is not a dish I would choose to serve on a hot summer day but would be perfect on a cool autumn evening after a hard day of working in the yard or a full day of activity. I like to drink a fruity Beaujolais with it.

➡ YIELDS 1 PIZZA

INGREDIENTS

½ c (75 g) Yukon Gold Potatoes, unpeeled, cut into ½-inch (13 mm) dice

2 tsp (10 g) salt

1 tbsp (14 g) unsalted butter

1 clove garlic, minced

5 oz (142 g) oiled Pizza Dough ball (page 17)

6 oz (168 g) Préférés de nos Montagnes cut into ½-inch (13 mm) slices at room temperature

¼ c (35 g) smoked bacon, cooked and cut into ½-inch (13 mm) pieces

¼ c (35 g) thinly sliced red onion

Freshly ground black pepper

Thinly sliced chives for garnish

NOTE: It will be easier to slice the cheese if it is well chilled. Époisses would also be an acceptable substitute.

DIRECTIONS

Put the potatoes in a small saucepan with 2 cups (480 ml) of water and 2 teaspoons (10 g) of salt. Bring to a simmer and cook until they are easily pierced with the tip of a paring knife. About 6 to 8 minutes. Drain and reserve. Keep them warm if possible.

Heat the butter in a small skillet over medium heat. When the butter just barely begins to sizzle, add the garlic and cook until it is translucent, about 2 minutes. Remove from the heat and reserve.

Clean the grill.

Lightly grease a metal work surface and the palms of your hands. Place the dough ball in the center of the surface and press down evenly with the palm of your hand. Working with both hands, start in the middle and spread the dough out with your palms while stretching the outer edges with your fingers. You should have an approximately 12 by 8 inch (30 x 20 cm) rectangle.

Lift up the edge farthest from yourself and slide your fingers under the dough. Move to the direct zone of your grill and place the bottom edge of the dough at the farthest point from you and pull the dough toward you to place on grill. Gently lift up 1 edge of the dough with the tongs to check for color. When you see some color setting in, lift the dough and give it a quarter turn with the peel. When the dough is sufficiently browned on the bottom, but not charred, remove it from the direct zone and flip it over onto the indirect zone. The bottom is now the top.

Drizzle with the butter and garlic and brush the crust evenly. Add the cheese slices, sprinkle the bacon, potatoes and onions all over and close the lid on the grill for 1-2 minutes to heat the toppings and start melting the cheese. Move the pizza to the direct side of the grill and rotate every 15 to 30 seconds. When the bottom is crispy, sprinkle with black pepper, garnish with the chives, slice and serve.

BRESAOLA, RACLETTE AND CORNICHON PIZZA

Where do we begin here? Raclette is a semi-firm cow's milk cheese that melts really well. Raclette is also the name of a dish that might have originated in Switzerland but is served in all sorts of Alpine areas nowadays and can often be seen in many restaurants to our north in Quebec. What Raclette is is what you wish to make out of it. During the winter we gather the family around the table with our Raclette machine (really just a broiler with a bunch of mini pans) and plates and bowls full of foods for us to put in the little pans and melt and broil the cheese over. The possibilities are endless and everyone usually customizes their own little pan. I am including the ingredients for a very simple but extremely tasty Raclette pizza here. Your own combinations are bound only by your imagination. Be sure the pizza dough is pressed out very thinly before placing on the grill. This is a great pizza to make when the summer evenings start turning a little crisper, and everyone can huddle around the fire and help make the pizza.

➔ YIELDS I PIZZA

INGREDIENTS

5 oz (142 g) oiled Pizza Dough ball (page 17)

5 oz (142 g) plus 1 oz (28 g) Raclette cheese (preferably grated but sliced will work)

9 small cornichons, cut in half lengthwise

4 pickled pearl onions, cut into 4 slices each

1½ oz (42 g) air-cured beef, very thinly sliced (Bresaola or Viande des Grisons)

1 tbsp (3 g) thinly sliced chives, for garnish

DIRECTIONS

Lightly grease a metal work surface and the palms of your hands. Place the dough ball in the center of the surface and press down evenly with the palm of your hand. Working with both hands, start in the middle and spread the dough out with your palms while stretching the outer edges with your fingers. You should have an approximately 12 by 8 inch (30 x 20 cm) rectangle.

Lift up the edge farthest from yourself and slide your fingers under the dough. Move to the direct zone of your grill and place the bottom edge of the dough at the farthest point from you and pull the dough toward you to place on grill. Gently lift up 1 edge of the dough with the tongs to check for color. When you see some color setting in, lift the dough and give it a quarter turn with the peel. When the dough is sufficiently browned on the bottom, but not charred, remove it from the direct zone and flip it over onto the indirect zone. The bottom is now the top.

When you turn over the pizza onto the indirect side of the grill, sprinkle the 5 ounces (142 g) of cheese evenly across the crust. Add the cornichons, pickled pearl onion slices and spread the meat all over the top. Sprinkle the remaining 1 ounce (28 g) of cheese around the pizza. Move the pizza to the direct side of the grill and crisp to just short of the desired doneness. Move the pizza to the indirect side of the grill and close the grill cover to make sure all the cheese is melted and the other ingredients are warm. If doing this on a single zone grill you will need to protect the bottom of the dough with the pizza peel. Move the pizza to the direct side for final crisping. Remove from the grill, sprinkle with the chives, slice and serve.

ADDITIONAL TOPPING RECOMMENDATIONS: thinly sliced cooked potatoes, duck prosciutto, ham, duck confit, grilled or roasted vegetables.

DUCK CONFIT, BLACK FIG, BLUE CHEESE AND BALSAMIC PIZZA

This pizza by far and away was the most popular pizza at our restaurant in Vermont. I have cooked this pizza in New England Barbecue Society Grilling contests and have consistently come in the top 3 places to help secure a number of grilling championships. My recipe for duck confit takes 3 days to complete, so I am suggesting you purchase yours. If you want to make your own, search on the Internet or a favorite country French cookbook for a recipe; there are plenty. Fresh figs in season are a wonderful substitute for the dried and poached ones I call for here (if using fresh figs just cut them crosswise and lay slices all around the pizza). This is also a great cold pizza in the morning on your ride to work.

 YIELDS I PIZZA

INGREDIENTS

5 oz (142 g) oiled Pizza Dough ball (page 17)

Extra virgin olive oil

¾ c (105 g) Pizza Cheese Blend (page 20)

1 leg of duck confit picked from the bone

⅓ c (43 g) Poached Black Figs (page 54)

¼ c (35 g) crumbled blue cheese

1 tbsp (3 g) sliced chives

Balsamic reduction (either store-bought or reduce the fig poaching liquid to a glaze)

DIRECTIONS

Lightly grease a metal work surface and the palms of your hands. Place the dough ball in the center of the surface and press down evenly with the palm of your hand. Working with both hands, start in the middle and spread the dough out with your palms while stretching the outer edges with your fingers. You should have an approximately 12 by 8 inch (30 x 20 cm) rectangle.

Lift up the edge farthest from yourself and slide your fingers under the dough. Move to the direct zone of your grill and place the bottom edge of the dough at the farthest point from you and pull the dough toward you to place on grill. Gently lift up 1 edge of the dough with the tongs to check for color. When you see some color setting in, lift the dough and give it a quarter turn with the peel. When the dough is sufficiently browned on the bottom, but not charred, remove it from the direct zone and flip it over onto the indirect zone. The bottom is now the top.

Drizzle with olive oil and brush the crust evenly. Sprinkle on the pizza cheese, scatter the duck confit and figs evenly and sprinkle on the blue cheese. Cover the grill for 1 minute or 2 to warm the duck and figs. Move to the direct side of the grill and rotate every 15 to 30 seconds to crisp the bottom. Remove from the grill, sprinkle the chives all over and drizzle balsamic glaze in ribbons across the whole pizza. Slice and serve.

(continued)

POACHED BLACK FIGS

➡ YIELDS 1½ CUPS (240 G)

INGREDIENTS

1 c (166 g) black figs, trimmed of tops and cut into quarters lengthwise

½ c (120 ml) dry red wine

½ c (120 ml) balsamic vinegar

½ c (100 g) granulated sugar

DIRECTIONS

Place all the ingredients in a saucepan and bring to a simmer for 7 to 10 minutes. Remove from the heat and let cool. When ready to use, remove the amount you need from the liquid and drain. Reserve the liquid and make the glaze or use it in a vinaigrette.

FIRE-ROASTED CORN, BRESAOLA AND TOMATO PIZZA

Bresaola is air-dried, salt-cured beef that is usually hung to dry for 2–3 months. It is very lean and tender and has a sweet taste with a musty aroma. When you cut it, slice it paper-thin and it will almost melt on your tongue. Roasting the sweet corn will bring a little nuttiness out of the kernels. Corn and tomatoes are generally in season around the same time so try to use a nice, fully ripened local tomato for this pizza. This is another summer favorite around my neck of the woods.

 YIELDS 1 PIZZA

INGREDIENTS

1 large ear of corn, shucked and silk removed

1 medium to large ripe tomato

Salt

Freshly ground black pepper

5 oz (142 g) oiled Pizza Dough ball (page 17)

¾ c (105 g) Pizza Cheese Blend (page 20)

Extra virgin olive oil

10–12 very thinly sliced pieces of Bresaola

4–5 basil leaves, torn into pieces, for garnish

DIRECTIONS

Grill the corn over a medium-high heat fire until it takes on a slight char, remove from the grill and cool. When the corn is cool enough to handle, remove the kernels from the cob and reserve. Reserve the cob for another use (corn stock perhaps).

Slice the tomato into 5 or 6 slices and season with the salt and pepper.

Clean the grill.

Lightly grease a metal work surface and the palms of your hands. Place the dough ball in the center of the surface and press down evenly with the palm of your hand. Working with both hands, start in the middle and spread the dough out with your palms while stretching the outer edges with your fingers. You should have an approximately 12 by 8 inch (30 x 20 cm) rectangle.

Lift up the edge farthest from yourself and slide your fingers under the dough. Move to the direct zone of your grill and place the bottom edge of the dough at the farthest point from you and pull the dough toward you to place on grill. Gently lift up 1 edge of the dough with the tongs to check for color. When you see some color setting in, lift the dough and give it a quarter turn with the peel. When the dough is sufficiently browned on the bottom, but not charred, remove it from the direct zone and flip it over onto the indirect zone.

Drizzle with olive oil and brush the crust evenly. Sprinkle the cheese all over, place the tomatoes on the pizza, add the corn, distributing evenly, and move the pizza to the direct side of the grill. Rotate the pizza every 15 to 30 seconds to crisp the bottom. When the bottom is crispy remove from the grill. Lay the sliced Bresaola all over, drizzle with olive oil and garnish with the torn basil leaves. Slice and serve.

SWEET SAUSAGE, RABE AND ROMANO PIZZA

This pizza is a take on the classic pasta dish Orecchiette with broccoli rabe, sausage and Pecorino Romano. This requires some advance preparation, but once you taste the synergy of the ingredients, the sweet, salty sausage, the bitterness of the rabe and the salty slight bitterness of the Romano, you will want to add this pizza to your list of "death row meals." I like to drink a full-bodied white wine with this pizza.

 YIELDS 1 PIZZA

INGREDIENTS

5 oz (142 g) oiled Pizza Dough ball (page 17)

Extra virgin olive oil

½ c (70 g) Pizza Cheese Blend (page 20)

½ c (20 g) Sautéed Broccoli Rabe (page 57)

4 oz (113 g) sweet Italian sausage removed from casing, cooked and crumbled

¼ c (35 g) grated Pecorino Romano

DIRECTIONS

Lightly grease a metal work surface and the palms of your hands. Place the dough ball in the center of the surface and press down evenly with the palm of your hand. Working with both hands, start in the middle and spread the dough out with your palms while stretching the outer edges with your fingers. You should have an approximately 12 by 8 inch (30 x 20 cm) rectangle.

Lift up the edge farthest from yourself and slide your fingers under the dough. Move to the direct zone of your grill and place the bottom edge of the dough at the farthest point from you and pull the dough toward you to place on grill. Gently lift up 1 edge of the dough with the tongs to check for color. When you see some color setting in, lift the dough and give it a quarter turn with the peel. When the dough is sufficiently browned on the bottom, but not charred, remove it from the direct zone and flip it over onto the indirect zone.

Drizzle with olive oil and brush the crust evenly. Sprinkle on the pizza cheese. Add the rabe, sausage and Romano. Close the lid of the grill for 1–2 minutes to help warm the toppings. Remember to check a few times to make sure the bottom isn't burning. Move to the direct side of the grill and rotate every 15 to 30 seconds to crisp up the bottom. Remove from the grill, drizzle with olive oil, slice and serve.

SAUTÉED BROCCOLI RABE

➡ YIELDS 1 QUART (950 ML)

INGREDIENTS

3 quarts (2.8 L) water

1 tbsp (8 g) salt

1 bunch broccoli rabe

2 tbsp (30 ml) extra virgin olive oil

2 garlic cloves, crushed and chopped

1 tsp (2 g) crushed red pepper flakes

2 tbsp (30 ml) dry white wine

DIRECTIONS

Bring 3 quarts (2.8 L) of water to a boil and add salt. Trim the ends of the broccoli rabe. When the water boils add the broccoli rabe and cook for 4 minutes. Strain the rabe and shower it with cold water to stop the cooking process. When the rabe is cool, cut it into ½ inch (13 mm) pieces.

Place a 10-inch (25.5 cm) sauté pan on medium-high heat. Add the oil, garlic and pepper flakes. When the garlic begins to turn light brown and the pepper flakes have given off their heat and turn the oil a reddish hue, add the rabe and toss in the pan with a spoon or some tongs, add the white wine and cook until the liquid is evaporated. Remove from the pan and cool. This recipe makes more than you need for one pizza but is a great addition to an antipasto platter, sausage and Provolone sandwich or mixed into a frittata.

SHAVED FENNEL, PROSCIUTTO AND ARUGULA PIZZA

We served a fennel and mixed green salad wrapped in prosciutto at our restaurant almost the entire time it was open. It was definitely a customer favorite. I took it off the menu, and the guests just kept asking for it. I put it back on the menu and it stayed until the last day we were open. The light licorice flavor of the fennel offsets the pepperiness of the arugula and the salty sweetness of the prosciutto balances it all out. It's a very refreshing salad and makes a great light pizza. In order to get the fennel shaved as thinly as needed you will probably want to use a mandoline. You could probably use a microplane with large blades, but I don't think it will provide the same textural feel.

➡ YIELDS 1 PIZZA

INGREDIENTS

5 oz (142 g) oiled Pizza Dough ball (page 17)

Extra virgin olive oil

½ c (70 g) Pizza Cheese Blend (page 20)

¾ c (65 g) loosely packed shaved fennel bulb

1 c (20 g) loosely packed baby arugula

Juice of half a lemon

5-7 thin slices of prosciutto

Freshly ground black pepper

DIRECTIONS

Lightly grease a metal work surface and the palms of your hands. Place the dough ball in the center of the surface and press down evenly with the palm of your hand. Working with both hands, start in the middle and spread the dough out with your palms while stretching the outer edges with your fingers. You should have an approximately 12 by 8 inch (30 x 20 cm) rectangle.

Lift up the edge farthest from yourself and slide your fingers under the dough. Move to the direct zone of your grill and place the bottom edge of the dough at the farthest point from you and pull the dough toward you to place on grill. Gently lift up 1 edge of the dough with the tongs to check for color. When you see some color setting in, lift the dough and give it a quarter turn with the peel. When the dough is sufficiently browned on the bottom, but not charred, remove it from the direct zone and flip it over onto the indirect zone.

Drizzle with olive oil and brush the crust. Sprinkle the cheese evenly over the pizza and move to the direct side of the grill. Rotate the crust every 15 to 30 seconds to crisp up the crust. When the crust is almost as crisp as you would like, move the crust to the indirect side of the grill. Working quickly, add the fennel shavings and the baby arugula, distributing evenly and trying to keep them a bit fluffy, sprinkle with the lemon juice and drizzle with olive oil. Place the prosciutto slices on top, trying not to overlap them, sprinkle with pepper, remove from the grill, slice and serve.

SHAVED BRUSSELS SPROUTS, BACON, PECORINO AND MOZZARELLA PIZZA

This pizza is inspired by the Brussels Sprouts and Pancetta Pizza at Motorino in New York City. Every time we are in NYC we get one of these incredible pizzas. The pizza at Motorino is served with peeled whole brussels sprouts leaves. The grilled version takes an extra step in shredding and lightly caramelizing the brussels sprouts to bring out their nutty flavor.

➜ YIELDS 1 PIZZA

INGREDIENTS

Extra virgin olive oil

12-15 medium-size brussels sprouts, stems trimmed and sliced thinly

Salt

Freshly cracked black pepper

5 oz (142 g) oiled Pizza Dough ball (page 17)

3 oz (85 g) fresh Mozzarella, sliced thinly

¼ c (35 g) plus 2 tbsp (17 g) grated Pecorino Romano

4 strips smoked bacon, cooked and cut into 1-inch (2.5 cm) pieces

DIRECTIONS

Heat 2 tablespoons (30 ml) of olive oil in a sauté pan on high heat. When it begins to smoke, add all the sliced brussels sprouts leaves. Lightly salt and pepper and toss in the pan until the edges begin to caramelize. Toss for another minute and then transfer to a bowl or plate.

Lightly grease a metal work surface and the palms of your hands. Place the dough ball in the center of the surface and press down evenly with the palm of your hand. Working with both hands, start in the middle and spread the dough out with your palms while stretching the outer edges with your fingers. You should have an approximately 12 by 8 inch (30 x 20 cm) rectangle.

Lift up the edge farthest from yourself and slide your fingers under the dough. Move to the direct zone of your grill and place the bottom edge of the dough at the farthest point from you and pull the dough toward you to place on grill. Gently lift up 1 edge of the dough with the tongs to check for color. When you see some color setting in, lift the dough and give it a quarter turn with the peel. When the dough is sufficiently browned on the bottom, but not charred, remove it from the direct zone and flip it over onto the indirect zone.

Drizzle with olive oil and brush the crust evenly. Distribute the Mozzarella evenly around the crust and sprinkle the ¼ cup (35 g) of Romano all around, add the bacon and then top with the shredded brussels sprouts leaves.

Close the cover for a minute to allow the brussels sprouts leaves to heat up. Alternatively you could leave the pizza on the peel over a 1 zone fire for a minute with the cover closed so as not to burn the bottom. Open the cover and move to the direct side of the grill and rotate every 15 to 30 seconds to crisp the bottom. Remove the pizza from the grill and drizzle some olive oil around. Sprinkle some salt, freshly cracked pepper and the remaining 2 tablespoons (17 g) of Romano, slice and serve.

BARBECUED PULLED PORK PIZZA

This pizza was inspired by a visit to my good friends Amy and Mike "the Legend" Mills who operate 17th Street Bar and Grill and OnCue Consulting in Murphysboro, Illinois. We needed a lunch idea to feed the 30 students who were in attendance. I was pretty sure there wasn't any shortage of grills around the warehouse at 17th Street (an amazing place that you should put on your list of places to visit), so I offered to make a couple of different grilled pizzas. Amy and Mike thought it was a great idea so we planned it for the next day.

We actually tried to buy the pizza dough from a local pizzeria, but they gave us the big no-go on that. Except for semolina and yeast, 17th Street would have everything we needed, so I would make the dough. We assembled all the ingredients and got set up in the 20-quart (19 L) electric mixer. I was handed the dough hook to get started except it wasn't the dough hook for that mixer. Long story short, I had to make the dough by hand—a 10-pound (4½ kg) batch of it. That was a nice morning workout. Everything turned out fine, and all the attendees and staff enjoyed the pizza.

 YIELDS 1 PIZZA

INGREDIENTS

½ c (120 ml) barbecue sauce

½ c (120 ml) Basic Tomato Sauce (page 21)

6 oz (170 g) barbecued pulled pork

5 oz (142 g) oiled Pizza Dough ball (page 17)

Extra virgin olive oil

1 c (140 g) Pizza Cheese Blend (page 20)

½ small red onion, sliced thinly across the grain

1 scallion, green part only, sliced thinly

DIRECTIONS

Place the barbecue and tomato sauces together in a bowl and mix well to combine.

Wrap the pork in a little packet of foil and place in a corner of the grill to prewarm.

Lightly grease a metal work surface and the palms of your hands. Place the dough ball in the center of the surface and press down evenly with the palm of your hand. Working with both hands, start in the middle and spread the dough out with your palms while stretching the outer edges with your fingers. You should have an approximately 12 by 8 inch (30 x 20 cm) rectangle.

Lift up the edge farthest from yourself and slide your fingers under the dough. Move to the direct zone of your grill and place the bottom edge of the dough at the farthest point from you and pull the dough toward you to place on grill. Gently lift up 1 edge of the dough with the tongs to check for color. When you see some color setting in, lift the dough and give it a quarter turn with the peel. When the dough is sufficiently browned on the bottom, but not charred, remove it from the direct zone and flip it over onto the indirect zone.

Drizzle with olive oil and brush the crust. Sprinkle on the pizza cheese, scatter the pulled pork all around and spoon the sauce all around the pizza. Sprinkle the red onion around and return the pizza to the direct side of the grill. Rotate the pizza every 15 to 30 seconds to make sure it doesn't burn. When the cheese is melted and the bottom is crispy (probably around 2 minutes, depending on the heat of your grill), remove the pizza, sprinkle the sliced scallions, slice and serve immediately.

GRILLED PORK AND ROSEMARY APPLESAUCE PIZZA

Growing up, pork chops and applesauce were always a family favorite. Sometimes my mother would fry them in a skillet or bake them in the oven after being coated in seasoned bread crumbs. There would always be a jar of applesauce on the table to accompany the pork chops. The applesauce recipe I have included here is very easy to make, and although there are better commercially made applesauces nowadays than when I was young, I encourage you to make this one. The rosemary adds a nice piney, savory hint to the flavor. It also works well as a condiment on sandwiches.

➡ YIELDS 1 PIZZA

INGREDIENTS

6 oz (170 g) butt-end pork tenderloin, trimmed of all fat and sinew

Salt

Freshly ground black pepper

5 oz (142 g) oiled Pizza Dough ball (page 17)

Extra virgin olive oil

¾ c (105 g) Pizza Cheese Blend (page 20)

½ c (120 g) Rosemary Applesauce (page 65) at room temperature

Thinly sliced flat-leaf parsley, for garnish

DIRECTIONS

Season the pork with salt and freshly ground black pepper. Place over a medium-heat fire and cook, turning constantly for about 8 minutes (130°F [54°C] on an instant-read thermometer).

Remove from the grill and let rest. Just before making the pizza, slice the tenderloin diagonally across the grain in ¼-inch (6 mm) slices (about 12 slices).

Clean the grill.

Lightly grease a metal work surface and the palms of your hands. Place the dough ball in the center of the surface and press down evenly with the palm of your hand. Working with both hands, start in the middle and spread the dough out with your palms while stretching the outer edges with your fingers. You should have an approximately 12 by 8 inch (30 x 20 cm) rectangle.

Lift up the edge farthest from yourself and slide your fingers under the dough. Move to the direct zone of your grill and place the bottom edge of the dough at the farthest point from you and pull the dough toward you to place on grill. Gently lift up 1 edge of the dough with the tongs to check for color. When you see some color setting in, lift the dough and give it a quarter turn with the peel. When the dough is sufficiently browned on the bottom, but not charred, remove it from the direct zone and flip it over onto the indirect zone.

Drizzle with olive oil and brush the crust. Sprinkle the cheese all over and add the sliced pork. Spoon dollops of the applesauce all over. Close the lid of the grill for 1 to 2 minutes to warm the pork. Move the pizza to the direct zone of the grill and rotate the pizza every 15 to 30 seconds to crisp the bottom. When the bottom is crispy, remove the pizza from the grill, drizzle with olive oil, sprinkle the parsley over, slice and serve.

ROSEMARY APPLESAUCE

Leave the skins on the apples when you cook them to give the sauce an appealing reddish color.

➡ YIELDS 1 CUP (240 ML)

INGREDIENTS

1 lb (454 g) Braeburn or Macintosh apples, cored, unpeeled and cut into 1-inch (2.5 cm) chunks

½ c (120 ml) apple cider

1 tsp ground cinnamon

3-inch (7 cm) sprig fresh rosemary

1 tsp (25 g) kosher salt

DIRECTIONS

Combine all of the ingredients in a medium pot and cook over medium heat until the apples are soft and most of the liquid has evaporated. Discard the rosemary sprig. If some of the rosemary leaves remain, it is okay. Transfer the apples to a food mill fitted with the medium disk and pass through the mill (or press the apples through a medium sieve). Discard the skins. Refrigerate in a covered container until ready for use. The applesauce will last 5 days refrigerated.

HAWAIIAN PIZZA

The Hawaiian pizza is one of those ubiquitous pizzas you see on a lot of pizza shop menus. It has a great combination of salty, sour and sweet. Light the tiki torches and get the mai tais flowing for this one.

 YIELDS 1 PIZZA

INGREDIENTS

1 tbsp (15 ml) cider vinegar

¾ c (180 ml) Basic Tomato Sauce (page 21)

5 oz (142 g) oiled Pizza Dough ball (page 17)

Extra virgin olive oil

½ c (70 g) shredded part skim Mozzarella

½ c (70 g) shredded Monterey Jack

3 oz (85 g) shaved cooked ham

⅓ c (50 g) fresh pineapple, cut into ¼ to ½ inch (6 to 13 mm) cubes

Thinly sliced scallions, for garnish

DIRECTIONS

Add the cider vinegar to the tomato sauce and stir to combine.

Lightly grease a metal work surface and the palms of your hands. Place the dough ball in the center of the surface and press down evenly with the palm of your hand. Working with both hands, start in the middle and spread the dough out with your palms while stretching the outer edges with your fingers. You should have an approximately 12 by 8 inch (30 x 20 cm) rectangle.

Lift up the edge farthest from yourself and slide your fingers under the dough. Move to the direct zone of your grill and place the bottom edge of the dough at the farthest point from you and pull the dough toward you to place on grill. Gently lift up 1 edge of the dough with the tongs to check for color. When you see some color setting in, lift the dough and give it a quarter turn with the peel. When the dough is sufficiently browned on the bottom, but not charred, remove it from the direct zone and flip it over onto the indirect zone.

Drizzle with olive oil and brush the crust. Sprinkle the Mozzarella and Jack cheese all over, spoon the tomato sauce in dollops around the pizza. Add the ham and pineapple and close the lid for a minute to warm the toppings. Move the pizza to the hot side of the grill and rotate every 15 to 30 seconds to crisp the bottom. When the bottom is crispy, remove from the grill, drizzle with olive oil, garnish with the scallions, slice and serve.

PORK THREE WAYS PIZZA

Pork, bourbon and more pork—what a way to get a party going. Here is a salty, sweet, smoky, silky seductive treat sure to lower any inhibitions. Be sure to have the Soppressata sliced as thinly as possible so it melts on your tongue as you eat it and also crumble the bacon and sausage finely so the flavors all blend together. Another bourbon? Yes, Ma'am.

 YIELDS I PIZZA

INGREDIENTS

5 oz (142 g) oiled Pizza Dough ball (page 17)

Extra virgin olive oil

¾ c (105 g) Pizza Cheese Blend (page 20)

¼ c (35 g) cooked smoked bacon, chopped fine

½ c (70 g) cooked sweet Italian sausage, chopped fine

½ c (120 ml) Basic Tomato Sauce (page 21)

7–9 very thinly sliced pieces of Soppressata

Thinly sliced flat-leaf parsley, for garnish

DIRECTIONS

Lightly grease a metal work surface and the palms of your hands. Place the dough ball in the center of the surface and press down evenly with the palm of your hand. Working with both hands, start in the middle and spread the dough out with your palms while stretching the outer edges with your fingers. You should have an approximately 12 by 8 inch (30 x 20 cm) rectangle.

Lift up the edge farthest from yourself and slide your fingers under the dough. Move to the direct zone of your grill and place the bottom edge of the dough at the farthest point from you and pull the dough toward you to place on grill. Gently lift up 1 edge of the dough with the tongs to check for color. When you see some color setting in, lift the dough and give it a quarter turn with the peel. When the dough is sufficiently browned on the bottom, but not charred, remove it from the direct zone and flip it over onto the indirect zone.

Drizzle with olive oil and brush the crust evenly. Spread the cheese all over the crust and add the bacon and sausage. Spoon small dollops of the tomato sauce around the pizza and move the pizza to the direct side of the grill. Rotate the pizza every 15 to 30 seconds to crisp the bottom. When the bottom is crispy remove the pizza, drizzle with olive oil and garnish with the parsley. Arrange the slices of Soppressata around the pizza, slice and serve.

PROSCIUTTO AND MELON GRILLED PIZZA

Melon wrapped in prosciutto has always been a favorite pass-around appetizer at all of our summer parties. Try to find a beautifully ripe Cavaillon melon or cantaloupe to use for this recipe. The deep fruity intensity and earthiness of cantaloupe plays off wonderfully with the salty sweetness of the prosciutto. A little drizzle of balsamic vinegar adds just the right touch of acidity. Try it with a chilled Chablis.

 YIELDS 1 PIZZA

INGREDIENTS

5 oz (142 g) oiled Pizza Dough ball (page 17)

Extra virgin olive oil

½ c (70 g) Pizza Cheese Blend (page 20)

½ c (70 g) thinly sliced cantaloupe or similar type of ripe melon (skin removed)

5–7 thinly sliced pieces of prosciutto

1 tbsp (15 ml) good quality balsamic vinegar

1 tbsp (3 g) thinly sliced fresh mint leaves

DIRECTIONS

Lightly grease a metal work surface and the palms of your hands. Place the dough ball in the center of the surface and press down evenly with the palm of your hand. Working with both hands, start in the middle and spread the dough out with your palms while stretching the outer edges with your fingers. You should have an approximately 12 by 8 inch (30 x 20 cm) rectangle.

Lift up the edge farthest from yourself and slide your fingers under the dough. Move to the direct zone of your grill and place the bottom edge of the dough at the farthest point from you and pull the dough toward you to place on grill. Gently lift up 1 edge of the dough with the tongs to check for color. When you see some color setting in, lift the dough and give it a quarter turn with the peel. When the dough is sufficiently browned on the bottom, but not charred, remove it from the direct zone and flip it over onto the indirect zone.

Drizzle with olive oil and brush the crust evenly. Sprinkle the cheese all over and spread the melon slices all around. Move the pizza to the direct side of the grill and rotate every 15 to 30 seconds until the bottom is crispy. When the bottom is crispy, move to the medium-low side of the grill, arrange the prosciutto slices around the pizza, drizzle with the balsamic and olive oil and garnish with the mint leaves. Slice and serve.

BUFFALO CHICKEN GRILLED PIZZA

Buffalo wings, buffalo chicken sandwiches and buffalo chicken pizzas seem to be everywhere these days. There is no reason to leave grilled pizza out of the party. More often than not those bar favorites are deep-fried, which I am certainly not opposed to. We are going to lighten our chicken up a bit by grilling it. Have some cold beer on hand to cool the flames.

 YIELDS 1 PIZZA

INGREDIENTS

4 oz (113 g) boneless, skinless chicken breast

Extra virgin olive oil

Salt

Pepper

¼ c (60 ml) hot sauce (I use Frank's)

5 oz (142 g) oiled Pizza Dough ball (page 17)

½ c (70 g) Pizza Cheese Blend (page 20)

¼ c (35 g) crumbled blue cheese

2 tbsp (30 ml) blue cheese dressing

2 tbsp (15 g) finely diced celery

Thinly sliced scallion, (green part only), for garnish

DIRECTIONS

Rub the chicken lightly with oil and season with salt and pepper. Place the chicken over a medium-heat fire on the grill. Cook the chicken, turning several times until an instant-read thermometer placed in the thickest part of the breast registers 165°F (74°C). Remove the chicken from the grill and let rest. When cool enough to handle, slice the chicken thinly in crosswise strips. Place in a bowl, add the sauce, toss to coat the chicken and reserve.

Clean the grill.

Lightly grease a metal work surface and the palms of your hands. Place the dough ball in the center of the surface and press down evenly with the palm of your hand. Working with both hands, start in the middle and spread the dough out with your palms while stretching the outer edges with your fingers. You should have an approximately 12 by 8 inch (30 x 20 cm) rectangle.

Lift up the edge farthest from yourself and slide your fingers under the dough. Move to the direct zone of your grill and place the bottom edge of the dough at the farthest point from you and pull the dough toward you to place on grill. Gently lift up 1 edge of the dough with the tongs to check for color. When you see some color setting in, lift the dough and give it a quarter turn with the peel. When the dough is sufficiently browned on the bottom, but not charred, remove it from the direct zone and flip it over onto the indirect zone.

Drizzle with olive oil and brush the crust evenly. Sprinkle the cheese blend and the blue cheese all over, add the chicken slices and close the lid of the grill for 1 minute to help rewarm the chicken. Move the pizza to the hot side of the grill and rotate every 15 to 30 seconds to crisp the bottom. When the bottom is crispy, remove the pizza, drizzle with the blue cheese dressing, add the celery and scallion, slice and serve.

GRILLED LAMB AND BLUE CHEESE PIZZA

Back in the early days of coming up in the ranks as a cook in Boston, Number 9 Park used to serve Lamb with Gorgonzola Fondue. It was one of my favorite appetizers in the city at the time. This is a pizzafied version of it. Try it with a young Valpolicella.

➡ YIELDS 1 PIZZA

INGREDIENTS

5 oz (142 g) lean lamb top round, trimmed of all sinew

Salt

Freshly ground black pepper

5 oz (142 g) oiled Pizza Dough ball (page 17)

Extra virgin olive oil

½ c (70 g) Pizza Cheese Blend (page 20)

2 oz (57 g) blue cheese (preferably Gorgonzola), crumbled

¼ c (35 g) cured Moroccan olives, finely chopped

Thinly sliced chives, for garnish

DIRECTIONS

Season the lamb with salt and pepper and cook over a medium-high heat fire turning constantly until rare to medium rare (125°F [52°C]), about 5 to 7 minutes. Remove to a plate and let it rest for about 5 minutes. Slice the lamb across the grain diagonally and set aside.

Clean the grill.

Lightly grease a metal work surface and the palms of your hands. Place the dough ball in the center of the surface and press down evenly with the palm of your hand. Working with both hands, start in the middle and spread the dough out with your palms while stretching the outer edges with your fingers. You should have an approximately 12 by 8 inch (30 x 20 cm) rectangle.

Lift up the edge farthest from yourself and slide your fingers under the dough. Move to the direct zone of your grill and place the bottom edge of the dough at the farthest point from you and pull the dough toward you to place on grill. Gently lift up 1 edge of the dough with the tongs to check for color. When you see some color setting in, lift the dough and give it a quarter turn with the peel. When the dough is sufficiently browned on the bottom, but not charred, remove it from the direct zone and flip it over onto the indirect zone.

Drizzle with olive oil and brush the crust. Sprinkle the pizza cheese around the crust. Add the blue cheese and place the lamb slices on the pizza. Scatter the olives and move to the hot side of the grill and rotate every 15 to 30 seconds until the bottom is crispy (about 1–2 minutes depending on the temperature of your fire). Remove the pizza from the grill, garnish with the chives, drizzle with olive oil, slice and serve.

SPICY SOPPRESSATA AND WILDFLOWER HONEY PIZZA

Soppressata is an Italian dried salami. If you can't find it then just use some good Genoa salami and when you grill it sprinkle a little cayenne pepper on the slices to spice it a bit.

➡ YIELDS 1 PIZZA

INGREDIENTS

8 very thinly sliced pieces of spicy Soppressata

5 oz (142 g) oiled Pizza Dough ball (page 17)

Extra virgin olive oil

¾ c (105 g) Pizza Cheese Blend (page 20)

¾ c (180 ml) Basic Tomato Sauce (page 21)

2 tbsp (30 ml) wildflower honey

Flaky sea salt (such as Maldon)

DIRECTIONS

Place the Soppressтта slices over the medium-high heat fire on a grill. Leave them there for 30 seconds, flip and then 30 seconds more, remove to a bowl and reserve.

Clean the grill.

Lightly grease a metal work surface and the palms of your hands. Place the dough ball in the center of the surface and press down evenly with the palm of your hand. Working with both hands, start in the middle and spread the dough out with your palms while stretching the outer edges with your fingers. You should have an approximately 12 by 8 inch (30 x 20 cm) rectangle.

Lift up the edge farthest from yourself and slide your fingers under the dough. Move to the direct zone of your grill and place the bottom edge of the dough at the farthest point from you and pull the dough toward you to place on grill. Gently lift up 1 edge of the dough with the tongs to check for color. When you see some color setting in, lift the dough and give it a quarter turn with the peel. When the dough is sufficiently browned on the bottom, but not charred, remove it from the direct zone and flip it over onto the indirect zone.

Drizzle with olive oil and brush the crust evenly. Sprinkle the cheese over the crust evenly, spoon the tomato sauce in dollops around the pizza and place slices of the Soppressata around the pizza. Drizzle the honey, ensuring each slice of Soppressata gets a bit of honey on it. Move the pizza to the direct side of the grill and rotate every 15 to 30 seconds until the bottom is crispy. Drizzle a little more olive oil around the pizza and sprinkle some salt over the pizza. Remove the pizza, slice and serve.

FRUITS OF THE SEA

Living on the east coast there is usually an abundance of seafood to be had. Lobsters, clams, crabs, tuna from local waters, shrimp from the Gulf and white anchovies from the Mediterranean all lend themselves to being partners with other ingredients on grilled pizzas. Try the award-winning Lobster, Pesto and Bacon Pizza, which was a secret-order item at our restaurant in Vermont. My version of the Pepe's White Clam Pizza will leave you wishing for more, and do try the somewhat challenging (for anchovy beginners) Pissaladière. The deep rich umami flavors on smoky crust will transport you to the French and Italian coastal border.

LOBSTER, PESTO AND BACON PIZZA

This is a pizza I created for a grilling contest that ended up becoming a sort of secret call-ahead item when we ran the Belted Cow. I showed one of our regulars a picture of the pizza from the contest, and he asked if he could have one the next day. Sure enough, he gets the pizza and one of our other regulars was at the bar and raised an eyebrow, and he was back with his wife the next night for one. I put a picture up on a social media site and people would call the restaurant about it. As long as I had a day's notice I could order the lobster and make it for them. I'm sure it will be a hit with your lobster-loving friends too. I like to keep one claw whole as a centerpiece for the pizza—it's also fun to see if anyone tries to grab that piece first.

➜ YIELDS 1 PIZZA

INGREDIENTS

½ c (120 ml) Basic Tomato Sauce (page 21)

¼ c (60 ml) heavy cream

2 tbsp (17 g) grated Parmesan cheese

4 oz (113 g) cooked lobster meat

5 oz (142 g) oiled Pizza Dough ball (page 17)

Extra virgin olive oil

¾ c (105 g) Pizza Cheese Blend (page 20)

2 slices cooked smoked bacon, cut into ½-inch (13 mm) pieces

2 tbsp (17 g) No Nut Pesto (page 80)

Thinly sliced chives, for garnish

DIRECTIONS

Purée the tomato sauce in a blender or food processor until it is smooth.

Add the heavy cream and Parmesan cheese to a small saucepan and warm over medium heat to melt the cheese. Add the lobster, stir to coat all the pieces and heat gently to warm the lobster through.

Lightly grease a metal work surface and the palms of your hands. Place the dough ball in the center of the surface and press down evenly with the palm of your hand. Working with both hands, start in the middle and spread the dough out with your palms while stretching the outer edges with your fingers. You should have an approximately 12 by 8 inch (30 x 20 cm) rectangle.

Lift up the edge farthest from yourself and slide your fingers under the dough. Move to the direct zone of your grill and place the bottom edge of the dough at the farthest point from you and pull the dough toward you to place on grill. Gently lift up 1 edge of the dough with the tongs to check for color. When you see some color setting in, lift the dough and give it a quarter turn with the peel. When the dough is sufficiently browned on the bottom, but not charred, remove it from the direct zone and flip it over onto the indirect zone.

Drizzle with olive oil and brush the crust evenly. Spread the cheese over the crust, spoon the tomato sauce all around the pizza and add the bacon. Drain the lobster from the cheese sauce and reserve the liquid. Arrange the lobster around the pizza and spoon a little bit of the cheese sauce on each piece of lobster (just enough for a thin coating). Move the pizza to the direct side of the grill and rotate every 15 to 30 seconds to crisp the bottom. When the bottom is crispy, remove from the grill, drizzle the pesto around the pizza, garnish with the chives, slice and serve.

NO NUT PESTO

➡ YIELDS ABOUT 1¼ CUPS (170 G)

INGREDIENTS

1 quart (0.9 L) water

2 tbsp (30 g) kosher salt

2 c (80 g) tightly packed basil leaves

1 garlic clove, cut into 3 pieces

½ c (120 ml) olive oil

¼ c (35 g) grated Parmesan cheese

¼ c (35 g) grated Pecorino Romano cheese

DIRECTIONS

Add salt to one quart (0.9 L) of water and bring to a boil in a medium saucepan. Prepare an ice bath to shock the basil. When the water boils, add all of the basil and submerge it. Cook for 2 minutes, drain and then put the basil in the ice bath to shock it. When the basil is cold, drain it from the water and lightly squeeze the remaining water out of it.

Put the basil in the cup of a blender with the garlic and add about ⅛ cup (30 ml) of the olive oil, just enough to get the basil to purée (add a little more if you need to). Add the cheeses to the blender and turn the blender to high, pour the remaining oil in a slow stream into the cup. Remove the pesto to a sealable container and refrigerate until needed. The pesto should keep in the refrigerator for 7 days.

SHRIMP FRA DIAVOLO PIZZA

Fra diavolo means "brother devil" in Italian. It usually refers to a spicy, tomato-based sauce served with seafood or pasta. Typically the sauce is cooked, but I like to use the Basic Tomato Sauce here to maintain the lightness of the pizza. Remember to taste a piece of the chile to see how hot it is to determine how much of it you want to use.

 YIELDS I PIZZA

INGREDIENTS

12 shrimp, size 16/20, peeled, deveined, tails removed and butterflied

1 tsp (3 g) kosher salt

1 tsp (3 g) cayenne pepper

1 tbsp (15 ml) extra virgin olive oil, plus more for pizza

5 oz (142 g) oiled Pizza Dough ball (page 17)

¾ c (105 g) Pizza Cheese Blend (page 20)

¾ c (180 ml) Basic Tomato Sauce (page 21)

1 small serrano or jalapeño chile pepper, sliced crosswise

6 medium basil leaves, torn

Thinly sliced flat-leaf parsley, for garnish

DIRECTIONS

Place the shrimp, salt, cayenne and olive oil in a bowl and toss to coat the shrimp. Place the shrimp on the grill over a medium-heat fire and cook turning until barely cooked through and opaque (about 5 minutes), remove the shrimp from the grill and cover with aluminum foil.

Clean the grill.

Lightly grease a metal work surface and the palms of your hands. Place the dough ball in the center of the surface and press down evenly with the palm of your hand. Working with both hands, start in the middle and spread the dough out with your palms while stretching the outer edges with your fingers. You should have an approximately 12 by 8 inch (30 x 20 cm) rectangle.

Lift up the edge farthest from yourself and slide your fingers under the dough. Move to the direct zone of your grill and place the bottom edge of the dough at the farthest point from you and pull the dough toward you to place on grill. Gently lift up 1 edge of the dough with the tongs to check for color. When you see some color setting in, lift the dough and give it a quarter turn with the peel. When the dough is sufficiently browned on the bottom, but not charred, remove it from the direct zone and flip it over onto the indirect zone.

Drizzle with olive oil and brush the crust evenly. Sprinkle the cheese around the crust and place the shrimp on the pizza. Spoon dollops of the tomato sauce around the pizza and add as much of the chile pepper as you like. Close the cover of the grill for 1 minute. Move the pizza to the direct side of the grill and rotate every 15 to 30 seconds to crisp the bottom. When the bottom is crispy, remove the pizza drizzle with olive oil, add the basil and parsley, slice and serve.

WHITE CLAM, THREE CHEESE, BACON AND CHILI FLAKES PIZZA

This pizza was inspired from the legendary pizza joint Pepe's in New Haven. I think this is one of their biggest sellers and for good reason. Tender briny sweet clams, smoky bacon and sharp cheese all blend together welcoming you to a great plate of linguini with clam sauce, except the linguini is replaced by a nice smoky charred pizza crust. No forks needed.

➡ YIELDS 1 PIZZA

INGREDIENTS

5 oz (142 g) oiled Pizza Dough ball (page 17)

Extra virgin olive oil

¾ c (105 g) Pizza Cheese Blend (page 20)

5 strips smoked bacon, cooked and cut into ½-inch (13 mm) pieces

½ c (120 ml) White Clam Sauce (page 83) or one small can of white clam sauce (such as Pastene)

Large pinch of thinly sliced parsley

Small pinch of crushed red chili flakes

¼ c (35 g) grated Pecorino Romano

DIRECTIONS

Lightly grease a metal work surface and the palms of your hands. Place the dough ball in the center of the surface and press down evenly with the palm of your hand. Working with both hands, start in the middle and spread the dough out with your palms while stretching the outer edges with your fingers. You should have an approximately 12 by 8 inch (30 x 20 cm) rectangle.

Lift up the edge farthest from yourself and slide your fingers under the dough. Move to the direct zone of your grill and place the bottom edge of the dough at the farthest point from you and pull the dough toward you to place on grill. Gently lift up 1 edge of the dough with the tongs to check for color. When you see some color setting in, lift the dough and give it a quarter turn with the peel. When the dough is sufficiently browned on the bottom, but not charred, remove it from the direct zone and flip it over onto the indirect zone.

Drizzle with olive oil and brush the crust evenly. Sprinkle on the cheese blend and bacon. Spoon the clam sauce all around the pizza, distributing it evenly. Sprinkle the parsley and a few chili flakes around and then sprinkle the extra Romano over the top. If the clam sauce was not kept warm, close the lid on the grill for a minute to help warm it. Move to the direct side of the grill and crisp up until desired doneness. The cheese and sauce should be bubbling a bit. Make this pizza just a little crisper to support the extra liquid. Remove the pizza from the grill, slice and serve. Be ready to make another cuz it's gonna go fast.

WHITE CLAM SAUCE

➡ YIELDS ½ CUP (120 ML)

INGREDIENTS

2 tbsp (30 ml) extra virgin olive oil

4 cloves garlic, chopped

½ tbsp (4 g) crushed red chili flakes

½ c (120 ml) dry white wine (Chablis/
Pinot Grigio)

½ c (70 g) fresh chopped clams
(substitute canned if necessary), juices
strained and reserved

2 tbsp (30 g) Beurre Manie (1 tbsp
[14 g] of softened unsalted butter
mixed with 1 tbsp [8 g] of flour)

DIRECTIONS

Heat a sauté or saucepan over medium-high heat. Add the oil, garlic and chili flakes and cook the garlic until it is translucent. Add the wine and let reduce 1 minute, add the reserved clam juice and then stir in the Beurre Manie. Bring to a boil, let thicken slightly, then add the clams and cook 30-45 seconds. Remove from heat. If you are using the sauce right away it is okay to leave it in the pan. If you are making it ahead, then remove the sauce from the pan and cool in the refrigerator.

PISSALADIÈRE

Pissaladière is a tart/pizza/focaccia that is made in and around Nice, France, and the Ligurian region of Italy. It generally consists of caramelized onions, tomato jam, oil-cured olives and anchovies. I have never really thought of a food/dish from the south of France as an umami bomb, but get ready because this is a mouthful. I use white anchovies because I like the salinity and just a touch of lightness they contribute to the dish. If you want to double down on the anchovy flavor, just add some anchovy paste or chopped anchovies to the caramelized onions. Don't let this pizza scare you away from trying it because it has anchovies on it. Make it without the anchovies and try a bite with just a little piece of anchovy on it. You will be amazed at the difference in taste. The caramelized onions do take a while to prepare, but they can be made days in advance and held in the refrigerator. This pizza generally isn't made with cheese, but I add a little bit of Parmesan to amp up the flavor even more.

 YIELDS 1 PIZZA

INGREDIENTS

¾ c (105 g) Caramelized Onions, chopped roughly (page 86)

¾ c (180 ml) Basic Tomato Sauce (page 21), reduced slowly in a pan to ⅓ c (71 ml)

5 oz (142 g) oiled Pizza Dough ball (page 17)

2 tbsp (17 g) very good quality Parmesan cheese

¼ c (35 g) oil-cured Moroccan olives, chopped

12 white anchovy fillets

Thinly sliced flat-leaf parsley, for garnish

Extra virgin olive oil

DIRECTIONS

Combine the onions and the reduced tomato sauce in a bowl and stir to incorporate the tomato sauce into the onions.

Lightly grease a metal work surface and the palms of your hands. Place the dough ball in the center of the surface and press down evenly with the palm of your hand. Working with both hands, start in the middle and spread the dough out with your palms while stretching the outer edges with your fingers. You should have an approximately 12 by 8 inch (30 x 20 cm) rectangle.

Lift up the edge farthest from yourself and slide your fingers under the dough. Move to the direct zone of your grill and place the bottom edge of the dough at the farthest point from you and pull the dough toward you to place on grill. Gently lift up 1 edge of the dough with the tongs to check for color. When you see some color setting in, lift the dough and give it a quarter turn with the peel. When the dough is sufficiently browned on the bottom, but not charred, remove it from the direct zone and flip it over onto the indirect zone.

Spread the onion and tomato mixture evenly across the whole pizza, sprinkle with the Parmesan cheese, scatter the olives and close the grill for about 1 minute to allow the onion mixture to get warmed up. Open the grill cover and place the anchovies around the pizza. Move the pizza to the direct side of the grill and rotate every 15 to 30 seconds to get the bottom nice and crispy. When the bottom is crispy, remove from the grill, garnish with the parsley and drizzle a little olive oil around the pizza. Slice and serve.

CARAMELIZED ONIONS

INGREDIENTS

1 tbsp (15 ml) extra virgin olive oil

2 tbsp (28 g) unsalted butter

2 large sweet onions, sliced lengthwise

2 tbsp (30 ml) water

Salt

DIRECTIONS

Heat the olive oil and butter in a large saucepan over medium-high heat. Add the onions and cook, stirring often until the onions soften and start to turn golden. Turn the heat down to medium and cook, stirring occasionally until the onions collapse completely and turn a rich, caramel color, about 30 minutes. When the onions are nearly done, add the water and scrape the brown bits from the pan stirring into the onions. Season with salt and set aside to cool.

LA PUTTANESCA PIZZA

Sugo alla puttanesca **(which in Italian literally means "sauce of the whore") is a tangy, slightly salty sauce found in southern Italian cooking. It is usually made with tomatoes, olives, capers, garlic and sometimes anchovies. This is a full-flavored pizza that your friends will love with a robust Nero d'Avola.**

➡ YIELDS 1 PIZZA

INGREDIENTS

Extra virgin olive oil

1 clove garlic, sliced thinly

5 oz (142 g) oiled Pizza Dough ball (page 17)

¾ c (105 g) Pizza Cheese Blend (page 20)

¾ c (180 ml) Basic Tomato Sauce (page 21)

1 tbsp (8 g) chopped black olives (such as gaeta)

1 tbsp (8 g) chopped green olives (such as castelvetrano)

1 tbsp (8 g) capers, drained and rinsed

9 white anchovy fillets (optional)

Thinly sliced flat-leaf parsley, for garnish

DIRECTIONS

Heat 1 tablespoon (15 ml) olive oil in a small skillet over medium heat, add the garlic and cook until translucent, about 2–3 minutes, remove from the heat and reserve.

Lightly grease a metal work surface and the palms of your hands. Place the dough ball in the center of the surface and press down evenly with the palm of your hand. Working with both hands, start in the middle and spread the dough out with your palms while stretching the outer edges with your fingers. You should have an approximately 12 by 8 inch (30 x 20 cm) rectangle.

Lift up the edge farthest from yourself and slide your fingers under the dough. Move to the direct zone of your grill and place the bottom edge of the dough at the farthest point from you and pull the dough toward you to place on grill. Gently lift up 1 edge of the dough with the tongs to check for color. When you see some color setting in, lift the dough and give it a quarter turn with the peel. When the dough is sufficiently browned on the bottom, but not charred, remove it from the direct zone and flip it over onto the indirect zone.

Drizzle with olive oil and brush the crust. Sprinkle the cheese all over the crust, spoon dollops of tomato sauce all around (remember not to spread the tomato sauce). Add the olives and capers and spoon the garlic and olive oil mixture all around. Move to the direct side of the grill and rotate every 15 to 30 seconds to crisp the bottom. When the bottom is crispy, remove the pizza from the grill, arrange the anchovy fillets all around, sprinkle with the parsley, slice and serve.

MARINATED GULF SHRIMP, ROASTED PEPPER AND MOZZARELLA PIZZA

Our good friend Tony O'Rourke makes this pizza for us when we are lounging around his backyard while I am busy invading his wine cellar. Tony likes to make the shrimp ceviche style by marinating raw shrimp in the morning. I am going to modify his version slightly for those that might not prefer to eat ceviche. I hope he doesn't mind and still lets me invade his wine cellar.

 YIELDS I PIZZA

INGREDIENTS

12 pieces cooked shrimp, 16/20 size, shells and tails removed and split lengthwise

2 tbsp (30 ml) extra virgin olive oil, plus more for the pizza

2 tbsp (30 ml) fresh lemon juice

1 clove garlic, minced

1 tsp (1 g) thinly sliced flat-leaf parsley

Salt

5 oz (142 g) oiled Pizza Dough ball (page 17)

3 oz (85 g) fresh Mozzarella, sliced thinly

1 roasted red pepper, peeled, seeded and cut into strips

1 tsp (3 g) crushed red chili flakes

DIRECTIONS

Combine the shrimp, 2 tablespoons (30 ml) olive oil, lemon juice, garlic and parsley and stir to coat the shrimp. Season lightly with salt. Cover and leave in the refrigerator for at least an hour to allow the shrimp to macerate in the juices.

Lightly grease a metal work surface and the palms of your hands. Place the dough ball in the center of the surface and press down evenly with the palm of your hand. Working with both hands, start in the middle and spread the dough out with your palms while stretching the outer edges with your fingers. You should have an approximately 12 by 8 inch (30 x 20 cm) rectangle.

Lift up the edge farthest from yourself and slide your fingers under the dough. Move to the direct zone of your grill and place the bottom edge of the dough at the farthest point from you and pull the dough toward you to place on grill. Gently lift up 1 edge of the dough with the tongs to check for color. When you see some color setting in, lift the dough and give it a quarter turn with the peel. When the dough is sufficiently browned on the bottom, but not charred, remove it from the direct zone and flip it over onto the indirect zone.

Drizzle with olive oil and brush the crust. Place the Mozzarella slices around the pizza, scatter the red peppers around and top the pizza all over with the shrimp, making sure at least half of the marinade juices make it onto the pizza. Close the lid of the grill for 1 minute to help warm the shrimp. Move the pizza to the direct side of the grill and rotate every 15 to 30 seconds to crisp the bottom, about 1 to 2 minutes. When the pizza is crisp and the cheese is melted, remove from the grill. Sprinkle some chili flakes around, slice and serve. Hopefully we will be drinking a really crisp and cold Frascati while the Amarone I nabbed from Tony's cellar gets a little air.

PORCHETTA TONNATO PIZZA

Vitello Tonnato is a well-known dish that originated in Piemonte. It is typically sliced, roasted veal that is served with a mayonnaise-like tuna sauce. Porchetta has so many different variations today that I don't think I could even begin to tell you what it is. Porchetta, at its simplest, is just roasted pig. I am going to use a little poetic license because I like the way Porchetta Tonnato sounds. Some of the best Vitello Tonnato that I have ever had was loin of veal that was grilled and sliced, still slightly warm and lightly sauced with the tuna sauce. I am replacing the veal with pork tenderloin, which has a veal-like texture when it is cooked medium rare to medium. Pork is about ¼ of the price of veal, so we'll be saving a little extra to splurge on a better bottle of wine. Feel free to use veal or if you are squeamish about medium-rare pork, just use some sliced roasted pork loin leftover from another meal.

 YIELDS I PIZZA

INGREDIENTS

6 oz (170 g) butt-end pork tenderloin, trimmed of all fat and sinew

Salt

Freshly ground black pepper

5 oz (142 g) oiled Pizza Dough ball (page 17)

Extra virgin olive oil

½ c (70 g) Pizza Cheese Blend (page 20)

¼ c (60 ml) Tonnato Sauce (page 91)

Thinly sliced chives for garnish

Freshly ground black pepper

DIRECTIONS

Season the pork with salt and freshly ground black pepper. Place over a medium-heat fire and cook, turning constantly for about 8 minutes (130°F [54°C] on an instant-read thermometer).

Remove from the grill and let rest. Just before making the pizza, slice the tenderloin across the grain diagonally in ¼ inch (6 mm) slices (about 12 slices).

Clean the grill.

Lightly grease a metal work surface and the palms of your hands. Place the dough ball in the center of the surface and press down evenly with the palm of your hand. Working with both hands, start in the middle and spread the dough out with your palms while stretching the outer edges with your fingers. You should have an approximately 12 by 8 inch (30 x 20 cm) rectangle.

Lift up the edge farthest from yourself and slide your fingers under the dough. Move to the direct zone of your grill and place the bottom edge of the dough at the farthest point from you and pull the dough toward you to place on grill. Gently lift up 1 edge of the dough with the tongs to check for color. When you see some color setting in, lift the dough and give it a quarter turn with the peel. When the dough is sufficiently browned on the bottom, but not charred, remove it from the direct zone and flip it over onto the indirect zone.

Drizzle with olive oil and brush the crust. Sprinkle the cheese all over and add the sliced pork. Move the pizza to the direct side of the grill and rotate every 15 to 30 seconds until the pizza is crispy. Remove from the grill and spoon the Tonnato Sauce all around, sprinkle with chives and some freshly ground pepper, slice and serve.

TONNATO SAUCE

INGREDIENTS

½ c (120 ml) mayonnaise

4 oz (113 g) good quality canned tuna in olive oil

¼ c (60 ml) extra virgin olive oil

1 tbsp (15 ml) lemon juice

DIRECTIONS

Place all of the ingredients in a blender and blend until smooth. Remove from the blender and store in a covered container in the refrigerator until ready to use. The sauce will keep in the refrigerator for 3-4 days.

CRAB LOUIS AND GRILLED GREEN TOMATO PIZZA

When I was the chef at the Harvest in Cambridge's Harvard Square, I put a late-summer appetizer on the menu of fried green tomatoes and crab Louis. It was a big hit with all the guests who ordered it. I like to add a little bit of hot sauce (I use Tabasco) for just a touch of acidic heat. Here is the grilled pizza inspired by it.

➡ YIELDS 1 PIZZA

INGREDIENTS

1 medium green tomato, sliced into ¼-inch (6 mm) slices

Extra virgin olive oil

Salt

Freshly ground black pepper

4 oz (113 g) fresh crabmeat

⅓ c (80 ml) Thousand Island dressing

5 oz (142 g) oiled Pizza Dough ball (page 17)

½ c (70 g) Pizza Cheese Blend (page 20)

Hot sauce, such as Tabasco (optional)

Thinly sliced chives, for garnish

DIRECTIONS

Lightly oil the tomato slices on both sides and season with salt and pepper. Place the slices over a hot fire on the grill and cook until you get a little char on them, about 2 minutes. Flip the tomatoes and grill 1 minute more. Remove from the grill and cool. When cool enough to handle, chop the tomatoes into ½ inch (13 mm) dice and reserve.

Clean the grill.

Place the crabmeat in a bowl and add the ¼ cup (60 ml) of Thousand Island dressing and stir gently to combine. Refrigerate until needed.

Lightly grease a metal work surface and the palms of your hands. Place the dough ball in the center of the surface and press down evenly with the palm of your hand. Working with both hands, start in the middle and spread the dough out with your palms while stretching the outer edges with your fingers. You should have an approximately 12 by 8 inch (30 x 20 cm) rectangle.

Lift up the edge farthest from yourself and slide your fingers under the dough. Move to the direct zone of your grill and place the bottom edge of the dough at the farthest point from you and pull the dough toward you to place on grill. Gently lift up 1 edge of the dough with the tongs to check for color. When you see some color setting in, lift the dough and give it a quarter turn with the peel. When the dough is sufficiently browned on the bottom, but not charred, remove it from the direct zone and flip it over onto the indirect zone.

When you turn over the pizza onto the indirect side, drizzle with olive oil and brush the crust. Sprinkle the cheese evenly all over the pizza and scatter the chopped tomatoes all over the pizza. Move the pizza to the direct side of the grill and rotate every 15 to 30 seconds until the bottom gets crispy. When the bottom is crispy, move to the indirect side of the grill and spoon the crab salad in little spoonfuls all over. Remove from the grill, sprinkle a few drops of Tabasco around, garnish with the chives, slice and serve.

CHERMOULA MARINATED SHRIMP GRILLED PIZZA

Chermoula is a marinade often found in dishes from Morocco, Tunisia and Algeria. It is a pungent marinade that works well with both fish and meat. It is a flavor combination you'll seriously crave. You'll understand what I mean after you taste it. Make the whole batch of marinade and use it the next time you grill some meat.

 YIELDS 1 PIZZA

INGREDIENTS

12 pieces of cooked shrimp, 16/20 size, tails removed and split in half lengthwise

¼ c (60 ml) Chermoula (page 95)

5 oz (142 g) oiled Pizza Dough ball (page 17)

Extra virgin olive oil

1 c (140 g) Pizza Cheese Blend (page 20)

¾ c (180 ml) Basic Tomato Sauce (page 21)

1 tbsp (3 g) coarsely chopped cilantro

DIRECTIONS

Place the shrimp in a bowl and add the Chermoula and let marinate in the refrigerator at least an hour.

Lightly grease a metal work surface and the palms of your hands. Place the dough ball in the center of the surface and press down evenly with the palm of your hand. Working with both hands, start in the middle and spread the dough out with your palms while stretching the outer edges with your fingers. You should have an approximately 12 by 8 inch (30 x 20 cm) rectangle.

Lift up the edge farthest from yourself and slide your fingers under the dough. Move to the direct zone of your grill and place the bottom edge of the dough at the farthest point from you and pull the dough toward you to place on grill. Gently lift up 1 edge of the dough with the tongs to check for color. When you see some color setting in, lift the dough and give it a quarter turn with the peel. When the dough is sufficiently browned on the bottom, but not charred, remove it from the direct zone and flip it over onto the indirect zone.

Drizzle with olive oil and brush the crust. Spread the cheese out evenly and add dollops of tomato sauce all around, add the shrimp all over the pizza and spoon any remaining marinade that the shrimp were in around the pizza. Close the lid of the grill and let sit for 1 minute to warm the shrimp a bit. Move the pizza to the direct side of the grill and rotate the crust every 15 to 30 seconds to crisp the bottom. When the bottom is crispy and the toppings are hot, remove the pizza from the grill, sprinkle with the cilantro, slice and serve.

CHERMOULA

INGREDIENTS

1 tbsp (15 g) kosher salt

1 tbsp (8 g) sweet paprika

1 tsp (3 g) smoked paprika

1 tsp (3 g) ground cumin

¼ tsp freshly ground black pepper

1 tbsp (9 g) finely chopped garlic

2 tbsp (8 g) finely sliced flat-leaf parsley

2 tbsp (8 g) coarsely chopped cilantro

1 tbsp (10 g) finely chopped lemon zest

1 tbsp (15 ml) fresh lemon juice

½ c (120 ml) extra virgin olive oil

½ c (120 ml) water

½ c (120 ml) tomato purée

DIRECTIONS

Whisk together the salt, paprikas, cumin and black pepper to combine. Add the garlic, parsley, cilantro, lemon zest and lemon juice, then whisk in the oil, water and tomato purée. Store in an airtight container in the refrigerator for up to 2 weeks.

GREAT WAYS TO GET YOUR VEGGIES!

Everybody needs their vegetables, right? What better way to deliver them but on a smoky, crispy, charred pizza crust? You have got to try the spring mix of morels and ramps with creamy Fontina. The first bundles of California asparagus arriving on the east coast are a harbinger of our own short but exciting asparagus season. Do try the Shaved Asparagus and Baby Swiss Pizza at the height of local asparagus season—you will be hooked. As with every other pizza in the book, don't limit yourself to what is written here. Explore, take chances and come up with your own flavor combinations.

SHAVED ASPARAGUS AND BABY SWISS PIZZA

This is one of the pizzas I look forward to in the springtime when California asparagus starts to arrive on the East Coast. Asparagus is probably my favorite vegetable (aside from bacon), and once we start getting the nice California crop, it is only a matter of weeks before we start getting some from our East Coast farms. I am particularly fond of the asparagus that is grown at Verrill Farm in Concord, Massachusetts. Go and search out the deeply purple and lightly green tinged stalks, they will change your asparagus world.

 YIELDS 1 PIZZA

INGREDIENTS

8 asparagus spears

5 oz (142 g) oiled Pizza Dough ball (page 17)

Extra virgin olive oil

1 c (140 g) Baby Swiss, shredded (regular Swiss is an acceptable substitute)

2 oz (57 g) fresh Mozzarella, drained and broken into little pieces

Sea salt

Freshly cracked pepper

DIRECTIONS

Break off the woody ends of the asparagus at the natural bending/breaking point. With a peeler, start at the top near the tip and peel the stalk lengthwise, giving a very little turn after each peel until all you have left is the tip in your hand. Take a paring knife and slice the tip in half. Reserve all in a bowl.

Lightly grease a metal work surface and the palms of your hands. Place the dough ball in the center of the surface and press down evenly with the palm of your hand. Working with both hands, start in the middle and spread the dough out with your palms while stretching the outer edges with your fingers. You should have an approximately 12 by 8 inch (30 x 20 cm) rectangle.

Lift up the edge farthest from yourself and slide your fingers under the dough. Move to the direct zone of your grill and place the bottom edge of the dough at the farthest point from you and pull the dough toward you to place on grill. Gently lift up 1 edge of the dough with the tongs to check for color. When you see some color setting in, lift the dough and give it a quarter turn with the peel. When the dough is sufficiently browned on the bottom, but not charred, remove it from the direct zone and flip it over onto the indirect zone.

Drizzle with olive oil and brush the crust evenly. Sprinkle on the Swiss and scatter the Mozzarella and asparagus strands all around the pizza. Move the pizza to the direct side of the grill and rotate every 15 to 30 seconds until the bottom is crispy. Remove the pizza from the grill, drizzle some olive oil and sprinkle some sea salt and cracked pepper around. Slice, serve and enjoy some springtime happiness.

NOTE: This pizza takes very well to the addition of crispy bits of ham or pancetta and a drizzle of hollandaise if you really feel motivated.

MOREL AND WILD LEEK GRILLED PIZZA

My good friend and confidant Jim Reiman is a great cook. This is his recipe using ramps and morels found foraging on his property. Cheers to you my friend, may we live long and prosper.

FROM JIM: Morels and wild leeks, or ramps, as they are widely known in Vermont and throughout New England, appear just about the same time in mid-spring. Harvested and cooked together, they offer a great combination of taste and texture. As a simple breakfast of scrambled eggs and toast, or tossed in pasta with a little butter and olive oil, morels and ramps certainly celebrate spring. They are also excellent as a topping on a grilled pizza with some Fontina cheese.

 YIELDS I PIZZA

INGREDIENTS

1 tbsp (14 g) butter

Extra virgin olive oil

1 c (66 g) fresh morels, woody stems removed, wiped clean and sliced lengthwise

8-9 small ramps, washed, bulbs removed and reserved for another purpose

Salt

Freshly ground black pepper

5 oz (142 g) oiled Pizza Dough ball (page 17)

1 c (140 g) shredded Fontina cheese

1 ramp leaf, thinly sliced, for garnish

DIRECTIONS

In a medium-size skillet heat the butter and 1 tablespoon (15 ml) olive oil over medium heat. When the butter begins to sizzle, add the morels, slice the ramps into ½ inch (13 mm) pieces and add to the morels. Cook the morels and ramps until the morels are tender (about 5 minutes), and most of the liquid has dissipated. Season with salt and pepper. Remove from the heat, cool and refrigerate until ready to use.

Lightly grease a metal work surface and the palms of your hands. Place the dough ball in the center of the surface and press down evenly with the palm of your hand. Working with both hands, start in the middle and spread the dough out with your palms while stretching the outer edges with your fingers. You should have an approximately 12 by 8 inch (30 x 20 cm) rectangle.

Lift up the edge farthest from yourself and slide your fingers under the dough. Move to the direct zone of your grill and place the bottom edge of the dough at the farthest point from you and pull the dough toward you to place on grill. Gently lift up 1 edge of the dough with the tongs to check for color. When you see some color setting in, lift the dough and give it a quarter turn with the peel. When the dough is sufficiently browned on the bottom, but not charred, remove it from the direct zone and flip it over onto the indirect zone.

Drizzle with olive oil and brush the crust evenly. Sprinkle the cheese on evenly and add the morel and ramp mixture. Close the lid on the grill for about 1 minute to let the mushrooms warm up, then move the pizza to the direct side of the grill. Rotate the pizza every 15 to 30 seconds to crisp the bottom. This should take 1-2 minutes depending on the heat of your grill. When the bottom is crispy, remove the pizza, drizzle with olive oil, garnish with the thinly sliced ramp leaves, slice and serve. Jim recommends serving with a slightly chilled Chianti.

TOMATO, GARLIC AND PECORINO ROMANO PIZZA

This pizza is an homage to the pizza strips I grew up eating in Providence and Johnston, Rhode Island. It was basically a thin focaccia sprinkled with a little Pecorino Romano cheese and a thick tomato and herb sauce. The pizza strips were sold cold from the bakery, not a pizzeria. Our relatives in Vermont always requested these when we went up for visits.

 YIELDS 1 PIZZA

INGREDIENTS

2 tbsp (30 ml) extra virgin olive oil, plus more for the pizza

2 cloves garlic, finely minced

1½ c (360 ml) Basic Tomato Sauce (page 21)

1 tsp (4 g) granulated sugar

Salt

Pepper

5 oz (142 g) oiled Pizza Dough ball (page 17)

¼ c (35 g) grated Pecorino Romano

Thinly sliced flat-leaf parsley, for garnish

DIRECTIONS

Place 2 tablespoons (30 ml) of olive oil in a small saucepan and heat slowly, add the garlic and cook until translucent. Add the tomato sauce and continue to cook over low heat until the sauce is reduced and very thick, around 30 minutes. You are trying to eliminate extra liquid and concentrate the tomatoes. Remove from the heat, add the teaspoon (4 g) of sugar and season with salt and pepper. You should have about 1 cup (240 ml) of sauce when finished.

Lightly grease a metal work surface and the palms of your hands. Place the dough ball in the center of the surface and press down evenly with the palm of your hand. Working with both hands, start in the middle and spread the dough out with your palms while stretching the outer edges with your fingers. You should have an approximately 12 by 8 inch (30 x 20 cm) rectangle.

Lift up the edge farthest from yourself and slide your fingers under the dough. Move to the direct zone of your grill and place the bottom edge of the dough at the farthest point from you and pull the dough toward you to place on grill. Gently lift up 1 edge of the dough with the tongs to check for color. When you see some color setting in, lift the dough and give it a quarter turn with the peel. When the dough is sufficiently browned on the bottom, but not charred, remove it from the direct zone and flip it over onto the indirect zone.

Drizzle with olive oil and brush the crust. Place the tomato sauce on the pizza and spread all over the crust evenly with the back of a spoon. Sprinkle the Romano all over. Move the pizza to the direct side of the grill and rotate every 15 to 30 seconds until the bottom is crispy. Remove from the grill, drizzle some olive oil over the pizza and garnish with the sliced parsley, slice and serve.

CHARRED TOMATOES, OLIVES AND GOAT CHEESE PIZZA

Charring tomatoes in a hot, dry skillet makes them smoky and flavorful. It can also help to intensify the flavor of a slightly underripe tomato. It's a technique I learned from the line cooks at La Campania when we would make salsa ranchera for a family meal. The char on the tomatoes plays well against the tangy goat cheese.

➡ YIELDS 1 PIZZA

INGREDIENTS

2 Roma tomatoes, cut crosswise into ½-inch (1.3 cm) pieces, tops and bottoms reserved for another use

Salt

Freshly ground black pepper

5 oz (142 g) oiled Pizza Dough ball (page 17)

Extra virgin olive oil

4 oz (113 g) soft goat cheese at room temperature

¼ c (35 g) cured Moroccan black olives, pitted and coarsely chopped

4–6 medium-size basil leaves, torn into pieces

DIRECTIONS

Place a cast-iron skillet over a hot fire on the grill and heat until smoking. Add the tomatoes in a single layer and cook until the bottom is charred. Flip the tomatoes with a spatula, season with salt and pepper and char the other side. Remove from the pan and reserve.

Lightly grease a metal work surface and the palms of your hands. Place the dough ball in the center of the surface and press down evenly with the palm of your hand. Working with both hands, start in the middle and spread the dough out with your palms while stretching the outer edges with your fingers. You should have an approximately 12 by 8 inch (30 x 20 cm) rectangle.

Lift up the edge farthest from yourself and slide your fingers under the dough. Move to the direct zone of your grill and place the bottom edge of the dough at the farthest point from you and pull the dough toward you to place on grill. Gently lift up 1 edge of the dough with the tongs to check for color. When you see some color setting in, lift the dough and give it a quarter turn with the peel. When the dough is sufficiently browned on the bottom, but not charred, remove it from the direct zone and flip it over onto the indirect zone.

Drizzle with olive oil and brush the crust evenly. Spread the goat cheese all over the crust with the back of a spoon, place the tomatoes on the pizza and sprinkle the olives on top. Move the pizza to the direct side of the grill and rotate every 15 to 30 seconds to crisp the bottom. When the bottom is crispy, remove the pizza from the grill, drizzle with olive oil, garnish with the basil, slice and serve.

GRILLED ZUCCHINI AND SHAVED PECORINO ROMANO PIZZA

I serve a warm, grilled zucchini and slivered almond salad with thin sheets of Pecorino Romano over the top of it. It's an amazingly good salad for a vegetable that I usually consider nondescript. You will want to barely cook the zucchini over a hot grill just enough to give it a little caramelization and retain its freshness. It makes for a great topping for a pizza.

➡ YIELDS 1 PIZZA

INGREDIENTS

6 oz (170 g) zucchini

Extra virgin olive oil

Salt

Freshly ground black pepper

1 tbsp (15 ml) fresh lemon juice

5 oz (142 g) oiled Pizza Dough ball (page 17)

¾ c (105 g) Pizza Cheese Blend (page 20)

¼ c (35 g) toasted slivered almonds

3-oz (85 g) wedge of Pecorino Romano

DIRECTIONS

Cut the ends off the zucchini and then cut into 4 even slices lengthwise. Brush the cut sides with a little olive oil and sprinkle with salt and pepper. Place the slices on a hot grill. Grill for 1 minute, then turn them over and grill them for 1 minute more. You want the zucchini to have a light tan/brown color to it. Grill a little longer on each side if necessary but keep the zucchini fairly firm. Remove from the grill and let cool. When the zucchini is cool, slice it on a long diagonal about ¼-inch (6 mm) wide. Toss in a bowl with the lemon juice and reserve.

Clean the grill.

Lightly grease a metal work surface and the palms of your hands. Place the dough ball in the center of the surface and press down evenly with the palm of your hand. Working with both hands, start in the middle and spread the dough out with your palms while stretching the outer edges with your fingers. You should have an approximately 12 by 8 inch (30 x 20 cm) rectangle.

Lift up the edge farthest from yourself and slide your fingers under the dough. Move to the direct zone of your grill and place the bottom edge of the dough at the farthest point from you and pull the dough toward you to place on grill. Gently lift up 1 edge of the dough with the tongs to check for color. When you see some color setting in, lift the dough and give it a quarter turn with the peel. When the dough is sufficiently browned on the bottom, but not charred, remove it from the direct zone and flip it over onto the indirect zone.

Drizzle with olive oil and brush the crust. Sprinkle the pizza cheese all over the pizza, add the zucchini slices spread out evenly. Sprinkle with the toasted almonds and close the lid of the grill to slightly warm the zucchini through. Move the pizza to the direct side of the grill and rotate every 15 to 30 seconds until the bottom is crispy. Remove the pizza from the grill, drizzle with olive oil and shave as much of the Pecorino Romano you want all over with a vegetable peeler, slice and serve.

MARINATED ARTICHOKE HEARTS, LEMON AND PECORINO ROMANO PIZZA

When I was the chef at La Campania, the owner was David Maione. His mother would make all sorts of amazing treats from slow-cooked broccoli rabe, marinated eggplant and marinated artichoke hearts. She was the type of cook who would actually take the time to peel the stalks of rabe before cooking them—a technique that changed the texture of the vegetable immensely. Her approach to artichoke hearts was similarly painstaking. For this pizza, I'll save you the trouble of peeling and poaching artichokes, which is very time consuming, by suggesting you use canned artichoke hearts. They won't be quite as good as David's mom's but will suffice for this pizza. This is a great pizza paired with one of my favorite cocktails, a Negroni.

 YIELDS I PIZZA

INGREDIENTS

½ c (70 g) artichoke hearts, drained and sliced thinly

1 lemon, zested and juiced, reserved separately

1 glove of garlic, minced

1 tbsp (3 g) thinly sliced flat-leaf parsley

2 tbsp (30 ml) extra virgin olive oil, plus more for the pizza

Salt

Freshly ground black pepper

5 oz (142 g) oiled Pizza Dough ball (page 17)

¾ c (105 g) Pizza Cheese Blend (page 20)

2 tbsp capers (17 g), drained

2 tbsp (17 g) pitted Gaeta olives, chopped fine

3-oz (84 g) wedge of Pecorino Romano (more than you need but it's hard to shave a smaller piece)

DIRECTIONS

Combine the artichokes, lemon juice, garlic, parsley and 2 tablespoons (30 ml) of olive oil in a bowl and stir. Season with salt and pepper and let marinate for at least 1 hour at room temperature.

Lightly grease a metal work surface and the palms of your hands. Place the dough ball in the center of the surface and press down evenly with the palm of your hand. Working with both hands, start in the middle and spread the dough out with your palms while stretching the outer edges with your fingers. You should have an approximately 12 by 8 inch (30 x 20 cm) rectangle.

Lift up the edge farthest from yourself and slide your fingers under the dough. Move to the direct zone of your grill and place the bottom edge of the dough at the farthest point from you and pull the dough toward you to place on grill. Gently lift up 1 edge of the dough with the tongs to check for color. When you see some color setting in, lift the dough and give it a quarter turn with the peel. When the dough is sufficiently browned on the bottom, but not charred, remove it from the direct zone and flip it over onto the indirect zone.

Drizzle with olive oil and brush the crust evenly. Sprinkle the cheese all over the crust. Scatter the artichoke hearts around the pizza, sprinkle the lemon zest, capers and olives over the pizza. Move the pizza to the direct side of the grill. Rotate the pizza every 15 to 30 seconds to crisp the bottom. When the bottom is crispy, move the pizza to the indirect side of the grill and using a vegetable peeler, shave the Pecorino Romano all around the pizza, remove from the grill, slice and serve.

GRILLED EGGPLANT, TOMATO AND FETA PIZZA

This is an easy variation of the Anything But Basic Pizza with the addition of grilled eggplant and feta cheese. Feta can be a bit salty depending on the variety you use so give it a taste before you use the entire recommended amount to be sure you do not oversalt your pizza.

➡ YIELDS I PIZZA

INGREDIENTS

6 oz (170 g) eggplant, sliced into ¼ inch (6 mm) rounds with the skin still on (about 9–10 slices)

Extra virgin olive oil

Salt

Freshly ground black pepper

5 oz (142 g) oiled Pizza Dough ball (page 17)

¾ c (105 g) Pizza Cheese Blend (page 20)

¾ c (180 ml) Basic Tomato Sauce (page 21)

¼ c (35 g) feta cheese, crumbled

Thinly sliced parsley, for garnish

DIRECTIONS

Brush the eggplant lightly with olive oil and season with salt and pepper, turn the eggplant slice over and repeat.

Place over a medium-high heat grill and cook until lightly caramelized on the bottom, then turn the eggplant over and do the same to the other side—probably about 2 to 3 minutes per side. The eggplant should be slightly soft in the middle. Remove from the grill and reserve.

Clean the grill.

Lightly grease a metal work surface and the palms of your hands. Place the dough ball in the center of the surface and press down evenly with the palm of your hand. Working with both hands, start in the middle and spread the dough out with your palms while stretching the outer edges with your fingers. You should have an approximately 12 by 8 inch (30 x 20 cm) rectangle.

Lift up the edge farthest from yourself and slide your fingers under the dough. Move to the direct zone of your grill and place the bottom edge of the dough at the farthest point from you and pull the dough toward you to place on grill. Gently lift up 1 edge of the dough with the tongs to check for color. When you see some color setting in, lift the dough and give it a quarter turn with the peel. When the dough is sufficiently browned on the bottom, but not charred, remove it from the direct zone and flip it over onto the indirect zone.

Drizzle with olive oil and brush the crust. Sprinkle the cheese, spoon dollops of the tomato sauce around the pizza (remember not to spread the sauce around). Add the eggplant but do not overlap the slices if you can avoid it. Move the pizza to the direct side of the grill and rotate every 15 to 30 seconds until the bottom is crispy. When the bottom is crispy, remove from the grill, sprinkle the feta and parsley all around and drizzle a little more olive oil. Slice and serve.

LAURA'S THAI VEGGIE PIZZA

This recipe was contributed by our longtime sous chef at the Belted Cow, Laura Schantz. Laura was always a bright and shiny presence in the kitchen and a joy to work with. When she first started working with us she ate more veal ragù than anyone I knew, then she turned to vegetarianism for some reason. Laura grilled many, many pizzas at the Belted Cow, and this is her contribution. Thanks for all the help, Laura!

 YIELDS 1 PIZZA

INGREDIENTS

1 broccoli crown, cut into florets

1 red bell pepper halved, seeds and ribs removed

4 oz (113 g) snap peas, stems and strings removed

½ small red onion, sliced thinly across the grain

Blended oil

Salt and pepper

5 oz (142 g) oiled Pizza Dough ball (page 17)

Extra virgin olive oil

Peanut Sauce (page 111)

½ c (70 g) whole-milk Mozzarella, shredded

2 oz (57 g) fresh Mozzarella, sliced thin

DIRECTIONS

Toss the vegetables with a liberal amount of blended oil and sprinkle with salt and pepper.

Place the vegetables over a medium-high heat fire. You want to give the vegetables some char and caramelization. Remove to a cookie sheet when they are done. Slice the peppers lengthwise.

Clean the grill.

Lightly grease a metal work surface and the palms of your hands. Place the dough ball in the center of the surface and press down evenly with the palm of your hand. Working with both hands, start in the middle and spread the dough out with your palms while stretching the outer edges with your fingers. You should have an approximately 12 by 8 inch (30 x 20 cm) rectangle.

Lift up the edge farthest from yourself and slide your fingers under the dough. Move to the direct zone of your grill and place the bottom edge of the dough at the farthest point from you and pull the dough toward you to place on grill. Gently lift up 1 edge of the dough with the tongs to check for color. When you see some color setting in, lift the dough and give it a quarter turn with the peel. When the dough is sufficiently browned on the bottom, but not charred, remove it from the direct zone and flip it over onto the indirect zone.

Drizzle with olive oil and brush the crust. Spread Peanut Sauce evenly over the crust and arrange the slices of fresh Mozzarella on the pizza. Arrange the vegetables all over the top, sprinkle the shredded Mozzarella all around. Close the grill for 1-2 minutes to help the cheese melt and to heat the vegetables. Move the pizza to the direct side of the grill and rotate every 15 to 30 seconds to crisp the bottom. When the bottom is crispy, remove the pizza, slice and serve.

PEANUT SAUCE

➡ YIELDS 1 CUP (240 ML)

INGREDIENTS

½ c (130 g) peanut butter

3 tbsp (45 ml) soy sauce

2 limes, zest removed and minced then juiced

½ c (120 ml) hoisin sauce

1 tsp (2 g) fresh ginger, peeled and minced

1 tbsp (15 ml) Mirin

1 tbsp (15 ml) Sriracha or other favorite hot sauce

1 tsp (6 g) salt

1 tsp (2 g) freshly ground black pepper

DIRECTIONS

Whisk all ingredients together in a small bowl and set aside to let the flavors come together.

ROASTED CAULIFLOWER AND PECORINO PEPATO PIZZA

This is another surprisingly simple pizza that yields an amazing amount of flavor. Pecorino Pepato is a semihard sheep's milk cheese that originated in Sicily. It has a sharp briny peppercorn flavor. If you can't find Pecorino Pepato, then freshly grated Pecorino Romano with very coarsely smashed black peppercorns can be substituted. Roasting the cauliflower brings out a ton of sweetness and a touch of earthiness. The cauliflower and cheese can also be served as a side dish.

 YIELDS I PIZZA

INGREDIENTS

5 oz (142 g) oiled Pizza Dough ball (page 17)

Extra virgin olive oil

¼ c (35 g) Pizza Cheese Blend (page 20)

¾ c (105 g) grated Pecorino Pepato

1 head Roasted Cauliflower (page 113)

2 large pinches of thinly sliced flat-leaf parsley

1 tbsp (3 g) finely sliced chives

Salt

Pepper

DIRECTIONS

Lightly grease a metal work surface and the palms of your hands. Place the dough ball in the center of the surface and press down evenly with the palm of your hand. Working with both hands, start in the middle and spread the dough out with your palms while stretching the outer edges with your fingers. You should have an approximately 12 by 8 inch (30 x 20 cm) rectangle.

Lift up the edge farthest from yourself and slide your fingers under the dough. Move to the direct zone of your grill and place the bottom edge of the dough at the farthest point from you and pull the dough toward you to place on grill. Gently lift up 1 edge of the dough with the tongs to check for color. When you see some color setting in, lift the dough and give it a quarter turn with the peel. When the dough is sufficiently browned on the bottom, but not charred, remove it from the direct zone and flip it over onto the indirect zone.

Drizzle with olive oil and brush the crust evenly. Sprinkle on the pizza cheese and distribute the Pecorino Pepato evenly around the pizza. Add the cauliflower and return to the direct side of the grill and rotate every 15 to 30 seconds to crisp the bottom. Remove the pizza, add the parsley and chives and drizzle with olive oil, slice and serve.

ROASTED CAULIFLOWER

➜ YIELDS ABOUT 2 CUPS (240 G)

INGREDIENTS

1 head cauliflower, cut into small florets

¼ c (60 ml) extra virgin olive oil

Salt and pepper

DIRECTIONS

Toss the cauliflower with the olive oil, salt and freshly cracked black pepper. Cook the cauliflower in a skillet over medium-high heat until caramelized but not too soft. Remove to a bowl and reserve. This will yield enough for 2 pizzas.

MUSHROOM AND FONTINA PIZZA

This is a simple but satisfying pizza for the mushroom lover in your family. I love the springy texture and earthy mustiness that mushrooms have, and they pair very well with the rich, nutty flavor and subtle fruity, grassy aroma of Fontina. Try this pizza with a bold red from Piemonte.

 YIELDS 1 PIZZA

INGREDIENTS

1 c (140 g) Mushroom Ragout (page 115)

5 oz (142 g) oiled Pizza Dough ball (page 17)

Extra virgin olive oil

1½ c (210 g) loosely packed shredded Fontina cheese

1 tbsp (8 g) grated Parmesan cheese

Thinly sliced flat-leaf parsley, for garnish

Thinly sliced chives, for garnish

DIRECTIONS

Heat the Mushroom Ragout in a pan on the grill and keep warm.

Lightly grease a metal work surface and the palms of your hands. Place the dough ball in the center of the surface and press down evenly with the palm of your hand. Working with both hands, start in the middle and spread the dough out with your palms while stretching the outer edges with your fingers. You should have an approximately 12 by 8 inch (30 x 20 cm) rectangle.

Lift up the edge farthest from yourself and slide your fingers under the dough. Move to the direct zone of your grill and place the bottom edge of the dough at the farthest point from you and pull the dough toward you to place on grill. Gently lift up 1 edge of the dough with the tongs to check for color. When you see some color setting in, lift the dough and give it a quarter turn with the peel. When the dough is sufficiently browned on the bottom, but not charred, remove it from the direct zone and flip it over onto the indirect zone.

When you turn over the pizza onto the medium-low side of the grill, drizzle with olive oil and brush the crust lightly. Sprinkle the Fontina cheese onto the crust and add the mushrooms all over. Move the pizza to the hot side of the grill and rotate every 15 to 30 seconds to crisp the bottom. When the bottom is crispy and the cheese is melted, remove from the grill, sprinkle with the Parmesan, drizzle with olive oil and garnish with the parsley and chives. Slice and serve.

MUSHROOM RAGOUT

→ YIELDS 1 CUP (140 G)

INGREDIENTS

1 tbsp (15 ml) extra virgin olive oil

2 tbsp (28 g) unsalted butter

2 cloves garlic, minced

2 c (240 g) assorted mushrooms
(example: shiitake, stems removed and
tops quartered; oyster, stemmed and
sliced lengthwise; cremini, sliced)

¼ c (60 ml) dry white wine

⅓ c (80 ml) Basic Tomato Sauce
(page 21)

Salt

Freshly ground black pepper

DIRECTIONS

Heat a large skillet over medium-high heat then add the oil and butter. When the butter begins to sizzle, add the garlic and cook 30 seconds. Add the mushrooms and cook until most of the juices have evaporated, add the wine and cook until most of the liquid is evaporated. Lower the heat to medium, add the tomatoes, season with salt and pepper and cook for 2 to 3 minutes. Remove from the heat, cool in the refrigerator. Keep covered in the refrigerator until ready to use. The mushrooms should last 5 days refrigerated.

GRILLED ASPARAGUS, SWEET ONION AND GOAT CHEESE PIZZA

I always look forward to cooking asparagus. I use it in risotto, make soup with it, shave it and sauté it with pasta, put it in omelets and many other things. I like to grill it to give it a nice smoky char, which plays well with its slightly bitter but sweet earthy flavor. I just wish the season would last longer. Try it with an unoaked Chardonnay from Oregon's Willamette Valley.

 YIELDS 1 PIZZA

INGREDIENTS

2½-inch (13 mm)-thick slices of a medium-size sweet onion, skin still on

Extra virgin olive oil

Salt

Freshly ground black pepper

6–8 medium pieces of asparagus, woody bottoms removed

1 tbsp (6 g) grated Parmesan cheese

5 oz (142 g) oiled Pizza Dough ball (page 17)

½ c (70 g) soft fresh goat cheese

Thinly sliced chives, for garnish

DIRECTIONS

Brush the onion slices lightly on both sides with oil and season both sides with salt and pepper. Place the onions on a medium-high heat spot on the grill and cook, turning a quarter turn every so often to promote an even char. When the bottoms are charred, flip the onions and repeat until the bottom is charred and the onions are slightly soft in the middle. Remove from the grill and let cool. Remove the skins, separate the rings and reserve.

Clean the grill.

Lightly oil the asparagus and season with salt and pepper and place on the grill perpendicular to the grates so they won't fall through. Roll the asparagus on the grill to get some char all over. When the asparagus have some nice char on them and they yield a bit to the touch, remove them from the grill and let cool. When the asparagus is cool enough to handle, slice diagonally into 2 inch (5 cm) pieces. Place in a bowl, sprinkle with the Parmesan and toss to lightly coat the asparagus pieces and reserve.

Clean the grill.

Lightly grease a metal work surface and the palms of your hands. Place the dough ball in the center of the surface and press down evenly with the palm of your hand. Working with both hands, start in the middle and spread the dough out with your palms while stretching the outer edges with your fingers. You should have an approximately 12 by 8 inch (30 x 20 cm) rectangle.

(continued)

Lift up the edge farthest from yourself and slide your fingers under the dough. Move to the direct zone of your grill and place the bottom edge of the dough at the farthest point from you and pull the dough toward you to place on grill. Gently lift up 1 edge of the dough with the tongs to check for color. When you see some color setting in, lift the dough and give it a quarter turn with the peel. When the dough is sufficiently browned on the bottom, but not charred, remove it from the direct zone and flip it over onto the indirect zone.

Drizzle with olive oil and brush the crust evenly. Add the goat cheese and spread all over with the back of a spoon, arrange the onion rings all around the pizza and add the asparagus pieces. Close the lid of the grill for about a minute to warm the toppings. Move the pizza to the direct side of the grill and rotate every 15 to 30 seconds to crisp the bottom. When the bottom is crispy, remove the pizza, drizzle with olive oil, add the chives, slice and serve.

TOMATO, MOZZARELLA AND PESTO PIZZA

Pesto can bring a bright flavor to any party. The cool, minty herbaceousness just seems to highlight anything it is paired with. Try this pizza with buffalo Mozzarella if you can—it has a lightly sour grassiness to it that regular milk Mozzarella doesn't have.

 YIELDS I PIZZA

INGREDIENTS

5 oz (142 g) oiled Pizza Dough ball (page 17)

Extra virgin olive oil

¾ c (105 g) Pizza Cheese Blend (page 20)

2 oz (57 g) thinly sliced Mozzarella

¾ c (180 ml) Basic Tomato Sauce (page 21)

2 tbsp (17 g) No Nut Pesto (page 80)

Thinly sliced flat-leaf parsley, for garnish

DIRECTIONS

Lightly grease a metal work surface and the palms of your hands. Place the dough ball in the center of the surface and press down evenly with the palm of your hand. Working with both hands, start in the middle and spread the dough out with your palms while stretching the outer edges with your fingers. You should have an approximately 12 by 8 inch (30 x 20 cm) rectangle.

Lift up the edge farthest from yourself and slide your fingers under the dough. Move to the direct zone of your grill and place the bottom edge of the dough at the farthest point from you and pull the dough toward you to place on grill. Gently lift up 1 edge of the dough with the tongs to check for color. When you see some color setting in, lift the dough and give it a quarter turn with the peel. When the dough is sufficiently browned on the bottom, but not charred, remove it from the direct zone and flip it over onto the indirect zone.

Drizzle with olive oil and brush the crust evenly. Sprinkle the pizza cheese all around, place the slices of Mozzarella on top and spoon dollops of the tomato sauce around. Drizzle the pesto all around and move the pizza to the direct side of the grill. Rotate the pizza every 15 to 30 seconds to crisp the bottom. When the bottom is crispy and the cheese is melted and bubbly, remove the pizza from the grill, drizzle with olive oil, garnish with parsley, slice and serve.

MOUNTAIN GORGONZOLA, CARAMELIZED ONION AND CANDIED WALNUT PIZZA

Gorgonzola, one of Italy's famous cheeses, is made in 2 ways—1 is a creamy, almost sweet type called Gorgonzola Dolce and the other is firmer, earthier and spicier (slightly peppery) called Mountain Gorgonzola or Gorgonzola Picante. I use the mountain version on this pizza because the flavors work well with the sweetness of the onions and the walnuts. It is a fairly pungently flavored cheese that happens to be one of my favorites. Try it on its own drizzled with a little honey.

 YIELDS 1 PIZZA

INGREDIENTS

5 oz (142 g) oiled Pizza Dough ball (page 17)

Extra virgin olive oil

½ c (70 g) Pizza Cheese Blend (page 20)

¼ c (35 g) Mountain Gorgonzola, crumbled

¼ c (60 g) Caramelized Onions (page 86)

2 tbsp (16 g) Candied Walnuts, chopped (page 121)

Thinly sliced chives, for garnish

DIRECTIONS

Lightly grease a metal work surface and the palms of your hands. Place the dough ball in the center of the surface and press down evenly with the palm of your hand. Working with both hands, start in the middle and spread the dough out with your palms while stretching the outer edges with your fingers. You should have an approximately 12 by 8 inch (30 x 20 cm) rectangle.

Lift up the edge farthest from yourself and slide your fingers under the dough. Move to the direct zone of your grill and place the bottom edge of the dough at the farthest point from you and pull the dough toward you to place on grill. Gently lift up 1 edge of the dough with the tongs to check for color. When you see some color setting in, lift the dough and give it a quarter turn with the peel. When the dough is sufficiently browned on the bottom, but not charred, remove it from the direct zone and flip it over onto the indirect zone.

Drizzle with olive oil and brush the crust evenly. Sprinkle the cheese all over, add the Gorgonzola and Caramelized Onions and move to the direct side of the grill. Rotate the pizza every 15 to 30 seconds to crisp the bottom. When the bottom is crispy, remove the pizza, drizzle with olive oil, sprinkle the walnuts and chives around, slice and serve.

CANDIED WALNUTS

→ YIELDS 1 CUP (120 G)

INGREDIENTS
1 c (120 g) walnut halves
¼ c (35 g) granulated sugar
1 tbsp (14 g) butter

DIRECTIONS

Heat a medium nonstick skillet over medium heat. Stir together walnuts, sugar and butter.

Stir frequently over medium heat for 5 minutes. When the sugar mixture starts melting, stir constantly until all sugar is melted and nuts are coated. Transfer immediately onto a sheet of parchment paper and separate the nuts right away. Using two spatulas will make this go faster. You don't want the nuts to turn into a clump. Once the coating hardens (5 to 7 minutes), transfer to a bowl and reserve.

THE SIX-SHOOTER PIZZA

I named this pizza after my favorite revolver, a Smith & Wesson stainless steel 6-inch (15 cm) .357 magnum that my parents gave me when I graduated from high school. It's a beautiful handgun and the 6 cheeses on this pizza make for a great target to devour. Try to use a good Gorgonzola to provide a little extra punch, just like the Six-Shooter does. I know it is in the vegetable section, so that is why I included chives.

 YIELDS I PIZZA

INGREDIENTS

5 oz (142 g) oiled Pizza Dough ball (page 17)

Extra virgin olive oil

½ c (70 g) Pizza Cheese Blend (page 20)

¼ c (35 g) sharp Provolone, shredded

¼ c (35 g) fresh Mozzarella, torn into small pieces

¼ c (35 g) Gorgonzola piccante, crumbled

Thinly sliced chives, for garnish

DIRECTIONS

Lightly grease a metal work surface and the palms of your hands. Place the dough ball in the center of the surface and press down evenly with the palm of your hand. Working with both hands, start in the middle and spread the dough out with your palms while stretching the outer edges with your fingers. You should have an approximately 12 by 8 inch (30 x 20 cm) rectangle.

Lift up the edge farthest from yourself and slide your fingers under the dough. Move to the direct zone of your grill and place the bottom edge of the dough at the farthest point from you and pull the dough toward you to place on grill. Gently lift up 1 edge of the dough with the tongs to check for color. When you see some color setting in, lift the dough and give it a quarter turn with the peel. When the dough is sufficiently browned on the bottom, but not charred, remove it from the direct zone and flip it over onto the indirect zone.

Drizzle with olive oil and brush the crust evenly. Sprinkle the Pizza Cheese Blend evenly as a base and scatter the Provolone, Mozzarella and Gorgonzola evenly across the pizza.

Close the lid on the grill to let the cheese start to melt, for about a minute, maybe a little longer. Move the pizza to the direct side of the grill and rotate every 15 to 30 seconds to crisp the bottom. When the bottom is crispy, move to the indirect side of the grill. If the cheese hasn't fully melted then close the lid of the grill for another minute and check. When the cheese is melted, remove from the grill, garnish with the chives, slice and serve.

RING OF FIRE PIZZA

This pizza was inspired by Pizzeria Verita, my favorite Neapolitan-style pizzeria in Burlington, Vermont. The acidic burn of the cherry peppers is where the name comes from. It also happens to be one of my favorite Johnny Cash songs.

➡ YIELDS I PIZZA

INGREDIENTS

5 oz (142 g) oiled Pizza Dough ball (page 17)

Extra virgin olive oil

½ c (70 g) Pizza Cheese Blend (page 20)

½ c (70 g) sharp Provolone, shredded

¾ c (180 ml) Basic Tomato Sauce (page 21)

¼ c (35 g) prepared hot red cherry peppers, sliced

4 medium-size basil leaves, torn into pieces

8-10 small fresh oregano leaves (do not substitute dried oregano; just omit the oregano if you can't find fresh)

DIRECTIONS

Lightly grease a metal work surface and the palms of your hands. Place the dough ball in the center of the surface and press down evenly with the palm of your hand. Working with both hands, start in the middle and spread the dough out with your palms while stretching the outer edges with your fingers. You should have an approximately 12 by 8 inch (30 x 20 cm) rectangle.

Lift up the edge farthest from yourself and slide your fingers under the dough. Move to the direct zone of your grill and place the bottom edge of the dough at the farthest point from you and pull the dough toward you to place on grill. Gently lift up 1 edge of the dough with the tongs to check for color. When you see some color setting in, lift the dough and give it a quarter turn with the peel. When the dough is sufficiently browned on the bottom, but not charred, remove it from the direct zone and flip it over onto the indirect zone.

Drizzle with olive oil and brush the crust evenly. Sprinkle the Pizza Cheese Blend and the Provolone all over the crust and spoon dollops of tomato sauce all around. Add the cherry peppers and move to the direct side of the grill. Rotate the pizza every 15 to 30 seconds to crisp the bottom. When the bottom is crisp, remove from the grill, drizzle with olive oil, add the basil and oregano, slice and serve.

TOMATO, ARUGULA AND AMARENA CHERRIES PIZZA

Amarena cherries are small, dark, slightly bitter sour cherries that are usually packaged in a heavy syrup. They are a classic ingredient for gelato and decorating chocolate cakes. I also find them quite capable of working alongside savory items. I served a duck and amarena cherry dish for a couple of years at La Campania that was a very good seller. There are good commercially produced brands available. I prefer the Fabbri brand, but I have also included a recipe here to make your own. Try replacing maraschino cherries with amarena cherries in your next cocktail.

 YIELDS I PIZZA

INGREDIENTS

5 oz (142 g) oiled Pizza Dough ball
(page 17)

Extra virgin olive oil

¾ c (105 g) Pizza Cheese Blend
(page 20)

2 oz (56 g) fresh Mozzarella, torn into
small pieces

¾ c (180 ml) Basic Tomato Sauce
(page 21)

1 tbsp (8 g) Amarena Cherries, drained
(page 125)

1 tbsp (15 ml) Amarena Cherries syrup
(page 125)

½ c (10 g) loosely packed baby
arugula

4 medium-size basil leaves, torn into
pieces

DIRECTIONS

Lightly grease a metal work surface and the palms of your hands. Place the dough ball in the center of the surface and press down evenly with the palm of your hand. Working with both hands, start in the middle and spread the dough out with your palms while stretching the outer edges with your fingers. You should have an approximately 12 by 8 inch (30 x 20 cm) rectangle.

Lift up the edge farthest from yourself and slide your fingers under the dough. Move to the direct zone of your grill and place the bottom edge of the dough at the farthest point from you and pull the dough toward you to place on grill. Gently lift up 1 edge of the dough with the tongs to check for color. When you see some color setting in, lift the dough and give it a quarter turn with the peel. When the dough is sufficiently browned on the bottom, but not charred, remove it from the direct zone and flip it over onto the indirect zone.

Drizzle with olive oil and brush the crust evenly. Sprinkle the cheese blend all over, add the Mozzarella and spoon dollops of the tomato sauce all over. Scatter the cherries and drizzle the syrup around. Move the pizza to the direct side of the grill and rotate every 15 to 30 seconds to crisp the bottom. When the bottom is crispy, add the arugula, drizzle with olive oil, sprinkle the basil around, slice and serve.

AMARENA CHERRIES

→ YIELDS ABOUT 3 CUPS (600 G)

INGREDIENTS

2 c (320 g) dried cherries

1 c (240 ml) dry red wine

2 c (402 g) granulated sugar

½ c (120 ml) water

¾ c (180 ml) amaretto

DIRECTIONS

Place all of the ingredients in a medium saucepan over medium heat and reduce by ⅓. Remove from heat, cool and store in a sealed container in the refrigerator until needed.

THE MASQUERADERS

Yes, the masqueraders, the sandwiches we all know and love, are quickly and easily turned into grilled pizza. Take the Ballpark Sausage Sandwich in its squishy bun with the ingredients all tucked inside and turn it into a crispy-crusted pizza where all the colors come alive. Now you have food and artwork to salivate over. If you have never had a Super Beef, you will definitely want to try out that pizza with its amazing combination of tender rare roast beef and mixture of horseradish and barbecue sauces that will instantly wake you out of a daze. Craving a Thanksgiving sandwich? Now you have a recipe to easily put together without having to roast the whole bird. If you have had it in a sandwich, I am pretty sure you can turn it into a pizza.

BALLPARK SAUSAGE PIZZA

Game day at Fenway Park is never really complete, actually doesn't get started, until you have had yourself a griddled sweet sausage and pepper sub standing on Lansdowne Street. Sure, you could just make a sub for your buddies—or you could demonstrate your grilling prowess by taking the same ingredients and transforming them into a grilled pizza. I always opt for the yellow mustard. Drink of choice? COLD BEER!

→ YIELDS 1 PIZZA

INGREDIENTS

1 tbsp (15 ml) extra virgin olive oil, plus more for the pizza

1 clove garlic, thinly sliced

1 red bell pepper, julienned

½ medium Spanish onion, julienned

Salt

Freshly ground black pepper

5 oz (142 g) oiled Pizza Dough ball (page 17)

1½ c (210 g) shredded Provolone

8 oz (227 g) cooked Italian sausage, skin removed and chopped coarsely

Yellow mustard (optional)

Thinly sliced parsley, for garnish

DIRECTIONS

In a medium saucepan heat the tablespoon (15 ml) of olive oil over medium heat. Add the garlic and cook until just translucent. Add the julienned pepper and onion and season with salt and pepper. Continue to cook until they begin to wilt and get soft but not mushy. Remove to a bowl and reserve.

Lightly grease a metal work surface and the palms of your hands. Place the dough ball in the center of the surface and press down evenly with the palm of your hand. Working with both hands, start in the middle and spread the dough out with your palms while stretching the outer edges with your fingers. You should have an approximately 12 by 8 inch (30 x 20 cm) rectangle.

Lift up the edge farthest from yourself and slide your fingers under the dough. Move to the direct zone of your grill and place the bottom edge of the dough at the farthest point from you and pull the dough toward you to place on grill. Gently lift up 1 edge of the dough with the tongs to check for color. When you see some color setting in, lift the dough and give it a quarter turn with the peel. When the dough is sufficiently browned on the bottom, but not charred, remove it from the direct zone and flip it over onto the indirect zone.

Drizzle with olive oil and brush the crust. Cover the crust with the Provolone, sprinkle the sausage all over and add the peppers and onions. Squirt the yellow mustard all over. Cover the grill for a minute to allow the ingredients to get warm. Move the pizza to the direct side of the grill and rotate every 15 to 30 seconds until crispy. Remove from the grill, sprinkle on the parsley, slice and serve.

THE SUPER BEEF PIZZA

In Massachusetts there are a lot of sandwich shops that specialize in a freshly roasted beef sandwich. My favorite is one from Nick's Famous Roast Beef in Beverly, called the Super Beef. It's a behemoth of a sandwich piled high with roast beef, tomatoes, onions, pickles, horseradish and barbecue sauces on a soft onion roll. After a long day and night of grilled pizza fun at my publisher Will's house, we were headed back to Vermont, and I knew we needed some food to absorb some of the fun before the ride. I watched my wife Katy (her first visit to Nick's) eat her sandwich in about 3 minutes flat without saying a word.

 YIELDS 1 PIZZA

INGREDIENTS

5 oz (142 g) oiled Pizza Dough ball (page 17)

Extra virgin olive oil

¼ c (60 ml) your favorite barbecue sauce (they use James River BBQ Sauce at Nick's)

1 c (140 g) shredded mild Cheddar cheese

½ c (120 ml) Basic Tomato Sauce (page 21)

4 oz (113 g) thinly sliced best quality rare roast beef

½ small red onion, sliced thinly across the grain

¼ c (35 g) dill pickles, cut into ¼-inch (6 mm) dice

¼ c (35 g) Horseradish Sauce (page 132)

DIRECTIONS

Lightly grease a metal work surface and the palms of your hands. Place the dough ball in the center of the surface and press down evenly with the palm of your hand. Working with both hands, start in the middle and spread the dough out with your palms while stretching the outer edges with your fingers. You should have an approximately 12 by 8 inch (30 x 20 cm) rectangle.

Lift up the edge farthest from yourself and slide your fingers under the dough. Move to the direct zone of your grill and place the bottom edge of the dough at the farthest point from you and pull the dough toward you to place on grill. Gently lift up 1 edge of the dough with the tongs to check for color. When you see some color setting in, lift the dough and give it a quarter turn with the peel. When the dough is sufficiently browned on the bottom, but not charred, remove it from the direct zone and flip it over onto the indirect zone.

Drizzle with olive oil and brush the crust. Spread half of the barbecue sauce all over the crust with the back of a spoon. Sprinkle the cheese evenly, drizzle tomato sauce, add the roast beef slices overlapping to completely cover the crust, add the onions and pickles. Drizzle the remaining barbecue sauce and the horseradish sauce all over and move the pizza to the direct side of the grill. Rotate the pizza every 15 to 30 seconds to crisp the bottom. When the bottom is crispy, remove from the grill, slice and serve.

HORSERADISH SAUCE

→ YIELDS 1¼ CUPS (300 ML)

INGREDIENTS

½ c (120 ml) good-quality mayonnaise

¼ c (60 ml) sour cream

2 tbsp (30 ml) fresh squeezed lemon juice

¼ c (35 g) prepared horseradish

2 tbsp (30 ml) extra virgin olive oil

1 tbsp (15 g) freshly ground black pepper

5 dashes Tabasco

DIRECTIONS

Add all of the ingredients together in a bowl and stir well to combine. Refrigerate until needed.

THE CUBANO PIZZA

I used to serve a Cuban quesadilla at our restaurant as a special now and then. It sold very well, as it should because it is basically just a rendition of the famous Cuban sandwich of Miami in a tortilla shell. I have included it here because it also makes a great pizza. I like to add tomatoes when they are in season and ripe.

 YIELDS | PIZZA

INGREDIENTS

5 oz (142 g) oiled Pizza Dough ball (page 17)

Yellow mustard

1½ c (210 g) shredded Swiss cheese

3 oz (85 g) of roast pork loin, thinly sliced

4 thin slices of boiled ham, shredded (alternatively, you could purchase shaved ham)

1 medium tomato, sliced thinly about 6-8 slices, optional

½ c (75 g) chopped dill pickles

DIRECTIONS

Lightly grease a metal work surface and the palms of your hands. Place the dough ball in the center of the surface and press down evenly with the palm of your hand. Working with both hands, start in the middle and spread the dough out with your palms while stretching the outer edges with your fingers. You should have an approximately 12 by 8 inch (30 x 20 cm) rectangle.

Lift up the edge farthest from yourself and slide your fingers under the dough. Move to the direct zone of your grill and place the bottom edge of the dough at the farthest point from you and pull the dough toward you to place on grill. Gently lift up 1 edge of the dough with the tongs to check for color. When you see some color setting in, lift the dough and give it a quarter turn with the peel. When the dough is sufficiently browned on the bottom, but not charred, remove it from the direct zone and flip it over onto the indirect zone.

Squirt a little mustard onto the shell and spread with the back of a spoon (enough for a very thin layer). Spread the cheese all over, lay the slices of roast pork around the pizza and add the shredded ham around. If using tomatoes, place the slices around the pizza, sprinkle with the dill pickles and squirt some yellow mustard around the pizza. Close the grill cover for 1 minute to help warm the toppings. Open the grill. Move the pizza to the direct side of the grill and rotate every 15 to 30 seconds until the bottom is crispy. Remove from the grill, slice and serve.

CHEESEBURGER PIZZA

We used to serve a very simple grass-fed Vermont beef cheeseburger with caramelized onions on a toasted English muffin when we ran the Belted Cow. Every now and then I would need a throwback to earlier days of burgers off the backyard grill with ketchup, pickles, mustard and onions, and every now and then one of the cooks would overcook a burger. There was no reason to let it go to waste and someone's mistake would usually make the staff happy at the end of the night when we would make a cheeseburger pizza. Nice cold beer at the end of the dinner shift never hurts either. For more burger ideas to turn into pizzas, check out Andy Husbands and Chris Hart's cookbook *Wicked Good Burgers*.

 YIELDS 1 PIZZA

INGREDIENTS

6 oz (170 g) ground beef, formed in a patty

Salt

Pepper

5 oz (142 g) oiled Pizza Dough ball (page 17)

1½ c (210 g) shredded Cheddar cheese (6 slices of American is a great substitute)

½ small red onion, sliced very thinly across the grain

⅓ c (43 g) chopped dill pickles

Ketchup

Yellow mustard

DIRECTIONS

Season the patty on both sides with salt and pepper and place on a medium-high heat grill. Cook approximately 3–4 minutes, then flip and cook another 3–4 minutes until the burger is medium rare to medium (about 130°F [54°C]). Remove from the grill. When it is cool enough to handle, crumble the burger and reserve.

Clean the grill.

Lightly grease a metal work surface and the palms of your hands. Place the dough ball in the center of the surface and press down evenly with the palm of your hand. Working with both hands, start in the middle and spread the dough out with your palms while stretching the outer edges with your fingers. You should have an approximately 12 by 8 inch (30 x 20 cm) rectangle.

Lift up the edge farthest from yourself and slide your fingers under the dough. Move to the direct zone of your grill and place the bottom edge of the dough at the farthest point from you and pull the dough toward you to place on grill. Gently lift up 1 edge of the dough with the tongs to check for color. When you see some color setting in, lift the dough and give it a quarter turn with the peel. When the dough is sufficiently browned on the bottom, but not charred, remove it from the direct zone and flip it over onto the indirect zone.

Spread the cheese all over and top with the crumbled burger, onions and pickles. Close the grill cover for 1 minute to warm up the toppings. Squirt ketchup and mustard all around and move to the direct side of the grill. Rotate the pizza every 15 to 30 seconds to crisp the bottom. When the bottom is crispy, remove, slice and serve.

STEAK LA PIZZAIOLA GRILLED PIZZA

This pizza is another variant of a sub I used to get from the deli near where I grew up. They would take a thin sirloin steak, sear it on the griddle, cover it with tomato sauce and Provolone and put it in the oven for the cheese to melt. Then they would settle it all into a sub roll. It works great as a pizza. I think it goes extremely well with a bracingly cold Lambrusco.

➡  YIELDS 1 PIZZA

INGREDIENTS

6 oz (170 g) New York sirloin steak about ½-inch (13 mm)-thick crosswise

Salt

Pepper

5 oz (142 g) oiled Pizza Dough ball (page 17)

Extra virgin olive oil

1½ c (210 g) shredded sharp Provolone

¾ cup (180 ml) Basic Tomato Sauce (page 21)

6 large basil leaves

DIRECTIONS

Moisten the steak with a little water and season with salt and pepper. Grill the steak to rare to medium rare and set aside to rest. After it has rested 3 minutes, slice it thinly (about ⅛-inch [3 mm] strips).

Clean the grill.

Lightly grease a metal work surface and the palms of your hands. Place the dough ball in the center of the surface and press down evenly with the palm of your hand. Working with both hands, start in the middle and spread the dough out with your palms while stretching the outer edges with your fingers. You should have an approximately 12 by 8 inch (30 x 20 cm) rectangle.

Lift up the edge farthest from yourself and slide your fingers under the dough. Move to the direct zone of your grill and place the bottom edge of the dough at the farthest point from you and pull the dough toward you to place on grill. Gently lift up 1 edge of the dough with the tongs to check for color. When you see some color setting in, lift the dough and give it a quarter turn with the peel. When the dough is sufficiently browned on the bottom, but not charred, remove it from the direct zone and flip it over onto the indirect zone.

Drizzle with the olive oil and brush the crust evenly. Spread 1 cup (140 g) of the Provolone cheese around the crust and then distribute the steak all across the crust. Top the pizza with the tomato sauce and sprinkle the remaining Provolone around evenly. Move the pizza to the direct side of the grill and rotate every 15 to 30 seconds until it gets to your desired crispness. Remove the pizza from the grill, place the basil leaves around and drizzle a little more olive oil around. Slice and serve.

PASTRAMI, SWISS AND YELLOW MUSTARD PIZZA

This pizza is a simple twist on one of my favorite sandwiches of hot pastrami and Swiss on a sub roll. The delicatessen on the corner in Providence, where I grew up, used to warm their pastrami up on the griddle, lay sliced Swiss over the top then squirt a liquid around it and cover it for a second to melt the cheese. I could hardly ever wait to walk back home to tear open the wax paper and chow down. My mother was a lunch monitor at our school once a week, and she would more often than not bring me a huge sub from Mr. D's Deli. It wasn't always a pastrami and Swiss, but whichever one it was, it was always welcome. I wasn't drinking beer back then in 3rd and 4th grades, but I highly suggest you ice down a couple of your faves to go with this pizza.

→ YIELDS I PIZZA

INGREDIENTS

2 oz (59 ml) of beer, preferably a lager

Yellow mustard

4 oz (113 g) thinly sliced smoked pastrami (preferably fatty, of course)

5 oz (142 g) oiled Pizza Dough ball (page 17)

Extra virgin olive oil

1½ c (210 g) shredded Swiss cheese

¼ c (35 g) red onion, thinly sliced across the grain

Freshly ground black pepper

DIRECTIONS

Put the beer and a squirt of mustard into a small saucepan, add the pastrami and place over a medium-heat area of the coals or fire to warm the pastrami. Don't boil it, just warm it up and tenderize it a little.

Lightly grease a metal work surface and the palms of your hands. Place the dough ball in the center of the surface and press down evenly with the palm of your hand. Working with both hands, start in the middle and spread the dough out with your palms while stretching the outer edges with your fingers. You should have an approximately 12 by 8 inch (30 x 20 cm) rectangle.

Lift up the edge farthest from yourself and slide your fingers under the dough. Move to the direct zone of your grill and place the bottom edge of the dough at the farthest point from you and pull the dough toward you to place on grill. Gently lift up 1 edge of the dough with the tongs to check for color. When you see some color setting in, lift the dough and give it a quarter turn with the peel. When the dough is sufficiently browned on the bottom, but not charred, remove it from the direct zone and flip it over onto the indirect zone.

Drizzle with olive oil and brush the crust evenly. Distribute a bit more than half the cheese onto the crust (you want good coverage). Remove the pastrami from the liquid with a fork or pair of tongs and spread around the pizza shell. Squirt the mustard all around the pizza and then top with the remaining cheese and red onion. Sprinkle some freshly cracked black pepper around and squirt some more mustard over the top. Cover the grill briefly to melt the top layer of cheese and then move the pizza to the direct side and rotate every 15 to 30 seconds to crisp the bottom. (I kind of like this one just a little less crispy and fold up the sides a little when I eat it.) Remove from the grill, slice and serve.

BLT&A GRILLED PIZZA

Bacon, lettuce and tomato sandwiches are one of the all-time greats, especially when you use top-grade ingredients.

The sandwich can easily be transformed into a pizza. I think one of the secrets to a great BLT is to oil and season the tomatoes just slightly in advance to help intensify their flavor. Be sure to use good-quality bacon and in this version, a nicely ripened avocado. I also replace the traditional lettuce with baby arugula for a little spicier flavor.

 YIELDS 1 PIZZA

INGREDIENTS

1 c (20 g) baby arugula, loosely packed

1 tbsp (15 ml) lemon juice

Salt

Pepper

5 oz (142 g) oiled Pizza Dough ball (page 17)

Extra virgin olive oil

1 medium tomato, sliced thinly and lightly dressed with olive oil, salt and pepper

4 strips of smoked bacon, cooked until just barely crisp

½ ripe avocado, flesh removed from skin and thinly sliced (do this just prior to making the pizza)

Good-quality mayonnaise such as Duke's or Hellman's (optional)

DIRECTIONS

Toss the arugula in a bowl with the lemon juice and season with salt and pepper.

Lightly grease a metal work surface and the palms of your hands. Place the dough ball in the center of the surface and press down evenly with the palm of your hand. Working with both hands, start in the middle and spread the dough out with your palms while stretching the outer edges with your fingers. You should have an approximately 12 by 8 inch (30 x 20 cm) rectangle.

Lift up the edge farthest from yourself and slide your fingers under the dough. Move to the direct zone of your grill and place the bottom edge of the dough at the farthest point from you and pull the dough toward you to place on grill. Gently lift up 1 edge of the dough with the tongs to check for color. When you see some color setting in, lift the dough and give it a quarter turn with the peel. When the dough is sufficiently browned on the bottom, but not charred, remove it from the direct zone and flip it over onto the indirect zone.

Drizzle with olive oil and brush the crust. Place the tomatoes around the pizza and add the bacon and avocado. Move the pizza to the direct side of the grill and rotate every 15 to 30 seconds until the bottom is crispy. Remove the pizza and scatter the arugula around. If you are using the mayonnaise, squeeze some lightly around the pizza. If you do not use the mayonnaise, then drizzle lightly with olive oil, slice and serve.

(continued)

THE REUBEN PIZZA

The Reuben strikes a perfect balance of corned beef, Swiss cheese, sauerkraut and Thousand Island dressing. It's a standard for most delis and diners. It's great any time of day. I like to drink a Doc Brown's Cel-Ray soda with it.

➡ YIELDS 1 PIZZA

INGREDIENTS

5 oz (142 g) oiled Pizza Dough ball (page 17)

2 tbsp (30 ml) Thousand Island dressing, plus more for garnish

1 c (140 g) shredded Swiss cheese

½ c (70 g) sauerkraut (I like the types sold in bags in the refrigerated section of the market.)

4 oz (113 g) thinly sliced corned beef

DIRECTIONS

Lightly grease a metal work surface and the palms of your hands. Place the dough ball in the center of the surface and press down evenly with the palm of your hand. Working with both hands, start in the middle and spread the dough out with your palms while stretching the outer edges with your fingers. You should have an approximately 12 by 8 inch (30 x 20 cm) rectangle.

Lift up the edge farthest from yourself and slide your fingers under the dough. Move to the direct zone of your grill and place the bottom edge of the dough at the farthest point from you and pull the dough toward you to place on grill. Gently lift up 1 edge of the dough with the tongs to check for color. When you see some color setting in, lift the dough and give it a quarter turn with the peel. When the dough is sufficiently browned on the bottom, but not charred, remove it from the direct zone and flip it over onto the indirect zone.

Spread the Thousand Island dressing all over the crust with the back of a spoon. Sprinkle the cheese all over, add the sauerkraut and arrange the corned beef on top. Drizzle some more Thousand Island dressing (as much as you like) and close the lid on the grill for 1 to 2 minutes to warm up the toppings. Move the pizza to the direct side of the grill and rotate every 15 to 30 seconds to crisp the bottom. When the bottom is crispy, remove from the grill, slice and serve.

THANKSGIVING PIZZA

I don't know about anyone else, but I am pretty crazy about Thanksgiving sandwiches. Layers of leftover turkey (always the dark meat for me), stuffing, squash, gravy and cranberry sauce. Here is a year-round lighter take on that using mostly items you get at the grocery store. You will have to buy more cranberry sauce than you will need, but you can use the rest in a cranberry port vinaigrette for salads.

 YIELD | PIZZA

INGREDIENTS

½ c (70 g) cooked butternut squash

1 tbsp (15 ml) maple syrup

¼ tsp grated nutmeg

Salt

Freshly ground black pepper

5 oz (142 g) oiled Pizza Dough ball (page 17)

Extra virgin olive oil

1 c (140 g) shredded Swiss cheese

3 oz (85 g) shaved good-quality smoked turkey

¼ c (35 g) cranberry sauce, preferably the chunky version

Thinly sliced chives, for garnish

DIRECTIONS

Purée the butternut squash and maple syrup in a food processor until smooth. Add the grated nutmeg and season to taste with salt and pepper. Remove the purée to a bowl and reserve.

Lightly grease a metal work surface and the palms of your hands. Place the dough ball in the center of the surface and press down evenly with the palm of your hand. Working with both hands, start in the middle and spread the dough out with your palms while stretching the outer edges with your fingers. You should have an approximately 12 by 8 inch (30 x 20 cm) rectangle.

Lift up the edge farthest from yourself and slide your fingers under the dough. Move to the direct zone of your grill and place the bottom edge of the dough at the farthest point from you and pull the dough toward you to place on grill. Gently lift up 1 edge of the dough with the tongs to check for color. When you see some color setting in, lift the dough and give it a quarter turn with the peel. When the dough is sufficiently browned on the bottom, but not charred, remove it from the direct zone and flip it over onto the indirect zone.

Drizzle with olive oil and brush the crust. Spread the cheese around the pizza and then add the smoked turkey shavings. Spoon dollops of the cranberry sauce and butternut squash purée around the pizza and move the pizza to the direct side of the grill. Rotate the pizza every 15 to 30 seconds until the bottom is crispy. Remove from the grill, add the chives, slice and serve.

MEATBALL GRILLED PIZZA

Lots of people enjoy a great meatball sub, and meatball pizzas are found on many pizza shop menus. It's just as easy to make a meatball grilled pizza. Usually when I make a batch of meatballs and gravy, there are lots of leftovers. You might as well use those leftovers for a fun night or afternoon of grilling pizza.

 YIELDS | PIZZA

INGREDIENTS

5 oz (142 g) oiled Pizza Dough ball (page 17)

Extra virgin olive oil

¾ c (105 g) Pizza Cheese Blend (page 20)

4-5 medium-size meatballs, sliced into ¼ inch (6 mm) slices

¾ c (180 ml) Basic Tomato Sauce (page 21)

½ c (70 g) shredded sharp Provolone

Thinly sliced flat-leaf parsley

DIRECTIONS

Lightly grease a metal work surface and the palms of your hands. Place the dough ball in the center of the surface and press down evenly with the palm of your hand. Working with both hands, start in the middle and spread the dough out with your palms while stretching the outer edges with your fingers. You should have an approximately 12 by 8 inch (30 x 20 cm) rectangle.

Lift up the edge farthest from yourself and slide your fingers under the dough. Move to the direct zone of your grill and place the bottom edge of the dough at the farthest point from you and pull the dough toward you to place on grill. Gently lift up 1 edge of the dough with the tongs to check for color. When you see some color setting in, lift the dough and give it a quarter turn with the peel. When the dough is sufficiently browned on the bottom, but not charred, remove it from the direct zone and flip it over onto the indirect zone.

Drizzle with olive oil and brush the crust evenly. Sprinkle the cheese over the crust evenly. Place the meatball slices on the pizza and spoon dollops of tomato sauce all around, ensuring some sauce touches each meatball. Sprinkle the Provolone over the meatballs and close the cover of the grill for about 1 minute to warm up the meatballs and toppings. Move the pizza to the direct side of the grill and rotate every 15 to 30 seconds to crisp the bottom. When the bottom is crispy and the cheese is melted and bubbly, remove from the grill, drizzle with olive oil, sprinkle with the parsley, slice and serve.

MORTADELLA AND FONTINA GRILLED PIZZA

One morning, while traveling in Italy, I was gathering goodies for the drive. I bought some Mortadella, Fontina and a crusty roll. I made a sandwich with a smear of mustard and put it in a paper bag and placed it on the dashboard of the car. It was a brilliantly sunny day and after driving for a few hours I pulled over for a snack break. The sun had warmed the sandwich through during the drive. I took a bite and the roll was still nice and crusty, the Mortadella had become slightly creamy and the Fontina was grassy and nutty. What a great combination. This is the grilled pizza inspired by that sandwich.

 YIELDS I PIZZA

INGREDIENTS

5 oz (142 g) oiled Pizza Dough ball (page 17)

Extra virgin olive oil

2 tbsp (30 ml) whole grain mustard

5 oz (142 g) Fontina, shredded (chill in the freezer for about 20 minutes to make shredding easier)

8-9 thin slices of Mortadella

1 c (20 g) loosely packed baby arugula

Freshly ground black pepper

DIRECTIONS

Lightly grease a metal work surface and the palms of your hands. Place the dough ball in the center of the surface and press down evenly with the palm of your hand. Working with both hands, start in the middle and spread the dough out with your palms while stretching the outer edges with your fingers. You should have an approximately 12 by 8 inch (30 x 20 cm) rectangle.

Lift up the edge farthest from yourself and slide your fingers under the dough. Move to the direct zone of your grill and place the bottom edge of the dough at the farthest point from you and pull the dough toward you to place on grill. Gently lift up 1 edge of the dough with the tongs to check for color. When you see some color setting in, lift the dough and give it a quarter turn with the peel. When the dough is sufficiently browned on the bottom, but not charred, remove it from the direct zone and flip it over onto the indirect zone.

Drizzle with olive oil and brush the crust. Spread the mustard in a thin layer all over the pizza, then add the Fontina. Move the pizza to the direct side of the grill and rotate every 15 to 30 seconds to crisp the bottom. When the bottom is almost as crispy as you would like it, move the pizza to the indirect side of the grill and arrange the slices of Mortadella all around it. Close the lid of the grill for about 1 minute to let the Mortadella warm through slightly. Check the bottom of the crust to see if it is as crisp as you like. Finish crisping on the hot side if needed, remove from the grill, add the arugula, drizzle with olive oil, sprinkle a little bit of black pepper, slice and serve.

PROSCIUTTO COTTO AND TALEGGIO GRILLED PIZZA

When you finish pulling a 12-hour shift in the kitchen, the last thing you usually want to do when you get home is cook. My wife Katy is the one who usually draws the short straw on that task. After unwinding for a little while, the reality that you haven't eaten all day starts to set in. Katy will normally make us some spaghettini with butter and grated Parm or a simple pita toasted with ham and cheese. Prosciutto Cotto is just the fancy way of saying cooked ham. Taleggio is a pungently aromatic but comparatively mild semisoft Italian cheese. If the aroma is too much for you, substitute Fontina or Cheddar. This is my version of Katy's pita. Try it with a well-chilled Soave.

 YIELDS 1 PIZZA

INGREDIENTS

5 oz (142 g) oiled Pizza Dough ball (page 17)

Extra virgin olive oil

4 oz (113 g) Taleggio, well chilled, then thinly sliced

3 oz (85 g) shaved cooked ham

Freshly ground black pepper

DIRECTIONS

Lightly grease a metal work surface and the palms of your hands. Place the dough ball in the center of the surface and press down evenly with the palm of your hand. Working with both hands, start in the middle and spread the dough out with your palms while stretching the outer edges with your fingers. You should have an approximately 12 by 8 inch (30 x 20 cm) rectangle.

Lift up the edge farthest from yourself and slide your fingers under the dough. Move to the direct zone of your grill and place the bottom edge of the dough at the farthest point from you and pull the dough toward you to place on grill. Gently lift up 1 edge of the dough with the tongs to check for color. When you see some color setting in, lift the dough and give it a quarter turn with the peel. When the dough is sufficiently browned on the bottom, but not charred, remove it from the direct zone and flip it over onto the indirect zone.

Drizzle with olive oil and brush the crust. Place the slices of Taleggio all over the pizza and scatter the ham over. Move the pizza to the direct side of the grill and rotate every 15 to 30 seconds to crisp the crust. When the bottom is crispy and the cheese is melted, remove from the grill, sprinkle with some black pepper, drizzle with olive oil, slice and serve.

CROSS-BORDER CONTENDERS

Food trucks, food carts and stalls are everywhere these days. More often than not you will see that these independent little businesses are combining and crossing ethnic cuisine borders. Don't let the notion that a cola-marinated steak combined with kimchi and cheese shouldn't be included on the same pizza. Give it a try and open up your eyes; after all, a pizza can be looked at as an unfolded taco or burrito. The opportunities are endless.

GRILLED SKIRT STEAK AND KIMCHI PIZZA

This pizza is a riff on some of the tacos I have had from Korean food trucks. The soy sauce and cola marinade give the beef a great char without having to cook the meat too much. Kimchi provides a great sour, fermented and spicy kick and the Jack/Cheddar mix brings it all together with its melty goodness. I know it sounds like a crazy combination, but the umami kick of it all together will have you wanting more. A lighter style of beer is my drink of choice with this pizza.

➡ YIELDS I PIZZA

INGREDIENTS

5 oz (142 g) skirt steak (you can substitute flap steak)

¼ c (60 ml) cola

¼ c (60 ml) light soy sauce

2 cloves garlic, crushed

Salt

Freshly ground black pepper

½ c (120 ml) Basic Tomato Sauce (page 21)

2 tbsp (30 ml) hoisin sauce

5 oz (142 g) oiled Pizza Dough ball (page 17)

Extra virgin olive oil

½ c (70 g) shredded Cheddar cheese

½ c (70 g) shredded Jack cheese

½ tbsp (15 g) sesame seeds

½ c (70 g) kimchi, drained and chopped coarsely (liquid reserved)

2 tbsp (30 ml) Spicy Mayo (page 149)

Thinly sliced green onion, for garnish

Cilantro sprigs (washed and shaken dry), for garnish

DIRECTIONS

Place the steak, cola, soy sauce and garlic in a resealable bag and marinate for 4 hours or up to 12 hours.

Remove the steak from the marinade, season with salt and pepper and cook over a hot fire on the grill, turning constantly for about 4 to 5 minutes. You want the meat to be rare to medium rare (about 120°F [49°C] on an instant-read thermometer). Remove the steak and let it rest. When cool enough to handle, slice the steak in thin strips against the grain and reserve.

Clean the grill.

Combine the tomato sauce and hoisin sauce in a blender or food processor and purée until smooth. Remove and reserve.

Lightly grease a metal work surface and the palms of your hands. Place the dough ball in the center of the surface and press down evenly with the palm of your hand. Working with both hands, start in the middle and spread the dough out with your palms while stretching the outer edges with your fingers. You should have an approximately 12 by 8 inch (30 x 20 cm) rectangle.

Lift up the edge farthest from yourself and slide your fingers under the dough. Move to the direct zone of your grill and place the bottom edge of the dough at the farthest point from you and pull the dough toward you to place on grill. Gently lift up 1 edge of the dough with the tongs to check for color. When you see some color setting in, lift the dough and give it a quarter turn with the peel. When the dough is sufficiently browned on the bottom, but not charred, remove it from the direct zone and flip it over onto the indirect zone.

Drizzle with olive oil and brush the crust evenly. Sprinkle the cheeses all over the pizza, sprinkle the sesame seeds and spoon the sauce around. Add the kimchi. Arrange the steak slices on the pizza and move to the direct side of the grill and rotate every 15 to 30 seconds to crisp the bottom. When the bottom is crispy, remove the pizza from the grill. Squirt the Spicy Mayo all over, garnish with the green onions and cilantro, slice and serve.

SPICY MAYO

INGREDIENTS

2 tbsp (30 g) Korean spicy chili paste
1 tbsp (15 ml) kimchi juice
¾ c (180 ml) mayonnaise

DIRECTIONS

Place the chili paste, kimchi juice and the mayonnaise in a bowl and stir to combine. Place in a squeeze bottle and refrigerate until needed. The Spicy Mayo will keep in the refrigerator for 7 days.

CARNE ASADA PIZZA

I love carne asada tacos. Actually, I love just about any taco or Mexican food. The flavors are fresh, bright and just make me feel good. I like to marinate the steak in cola to give the steak a nice caramel coating when grilling. Charring the ingredients for the salsa ranchera gives it a nice smoky contrast to the acidity of the lime juice. Kick back with a cold Modelo Especial or Paloma and enjoy the day. You might as well grab enough ingredients to make a few of these because they go fast.

 YIELDS 1 PIZZA

INGREDIENTS

5 oz (140 g) skirt or flap steak

¼ c (60 ml) cola

¼ c (35 g) chopped red onion

Salt

Freshly ground black pepper

5 oz (142 g) oiled Pizza Dough ball (page 17)

Extra virgin olive oil

¼ c (35 g) Refried Beans (page 151)

¾ c (105 g) shredded Monterey Jack cheese

½ c (115 g) Salsa Ranchera (page 151)

¼ c (35 g) Cotija cheese, crumbled

Cilantro sprigs, for garnish (be sure to wash them of any dirt)

DIRECTIONS

Place the steak in a resealable bag, add the cola and the chopped onion and marinate for 4 hours or up to 12 hours.

Remove the steak from the marinade, season with salt and pepper and cook over a high-heat fire on the grill, turning constantly for about 4 to 5 minutes. You want the meat to be rare to medium rare (about 120°F [49°C] on an instant-read thermometer). Remove the steak and let rest, when cool enough to handle, slice the steak in thin strips across the grain and reserve.

Clean the grill.

Lightly grease a metal work surface and the palms of your hands. Place the dough ball in the center of the surface and press down evenly with the palm of your hand. Working with both hands, start in the middle and spread the dough out with your palms while stretching the outer edges with your fingers. You should have an approximately 12 by 8 inch (30 x 20 cm) rectangle.

Lift up the edge farthest from yourself and slide your fingers under the dough. Move to the direct zone of your grill and place the bottom edge of the dough at the farthest point from you and pull the dough toward you to place on grill. Gently lift up 1 edge of the dough with the tongs to check for color. When you see some color setting in, lift the dough and give it a quarter turn with the peel. When the dough is sufficiently browned on the bottom, but not charred, remove it from the direct zone and flip it over onto the indirect zone.

Drizzle with olive oil, add the Refried Beans and spread all over the crust with the back of a spoon. Sprinkle the Monterey Jack cheese all over, arrange the steak slices on the pizza, spoon salsa (enough to cover each bite) and sprinkle the Cotija cheese over the top. Close the lid of the grill for 1 minute to help rewarm the steak. Move the pizza to the direct side of the grill and rotate every 15 to 30 seconds to crisp the bottom. When the bottom is crisp, remove from the grill, garnish all over the pizza with the cilantro sprigs, slice and serve.

REFRIED BEANS

➜ YIELDS 1¹/₂ CUPS (360 G)

INGREDIENTS

1 tbsp (14 g) lard (if you can't find lard, use unsalted butter)

½ c (120 g) Caramelized Onions, chopped (page 86)

8 oz (227 g) cooked black beans, drained and rinsed

¼ c (60 ml) water

DIRECTIONS

In a small saucepan heat the lard over medium heat, add the onions, stir for one minute, add the beans and ¼ cup (60 ml) of water and cook for 4 to 5 minutes. Transfer the mixture to the bowl of a food processor and purée until smooth, remove from the bowl and reserve until ready to use.

SALSA RANCHERA

➜ YIELDS 1 CUP (230 G)

INGREDIENTS

2 Roma tomatoes, cut in half lengthwise

½ red onion, peeled and cut in half crosswise

1 poblano pepper, cut in half lengthwise and seeded

1 medium jalapeño, stem removed

½ c (8 g) loosely packed cilantro, stems and leaves (make sure they are washed)

¼ c (60 ml) fresh lime juice

Hot sauce

Salt

Freshly ground black pepper

DIRECTIONS

Heat a medium-size cast-iron skillet over a high-heat fire. When the pan is smoking, add the tomatoes and the onion cut-side down, the poblano halves cut-side up, and the jalapeño. Cook over high heat to char all the vegetables. When the tomatoes are charred, flip them to char the skins, turn the jalapeno to char it all around. When all the vegetables are charred, remove from the fire and pour into a blender, add the cilantro and lime juice and a few sprinkles of hot sauce. Blend the vegetables until they are almost smooth, remove, season with salt and pepper, add more hot sauce if you like and reserve until ready to use.

KALE, CHORIZO AND MANCHEGO PIZZA

Kale, it's everywhere and highly regarded for its health benefits. I see people puréeing it with beets and apples, making kale chips, kale soup and so on. I personally love kale and oftentimes will make a kale salad or do a quick sauté with it. My wife Katy eats more salad than anybody I have ever seen; I guess that's what former Olympians do. She dreamed up this kale pizza one afternoon after staring at the ingredients in the crisper. Manchego is a Spanish sheep's milk cheese with an almond-like nuttiness to it, and the chorizo brings a little spicy meat action to the party. Might as well try to eat partially healthy sometime. Don't forget the health benefits of red wine either and try this with a Rioja or Tempranillo.

 YIELDS | PIZZA

INGREDIENTS

2 tbsp (30 ml) Spanish sherry vinegar

1 tbsp (15 ml) extra virgin olive oil, plus more for the pizza

2 c (134 g) green or black kale, shredded

Salt

Freshly ground black pepper

5 oz (142 g) oiled Pizza Dough ball (page 17)

¾ c (105 g) shredded Manchego, plus 2 tbsp (17 g) more for garnish

¼ c (35 g) cooked chorizo, crumbled

DIRECTIONS

Whisk together the vinegar and 1 tablespoon (15 ml) olive oil in a small bowl. Place the kale in a bowl, season with salt and pepper, pour the oil and vinegar mixture over the kale and toss the leaves to coat with the dressing. Set aside.

Lightly grease a metal work surface and the palms of your hands. Place the dough ball in the center of the surface and press down evenly with the palm of your hand. Working with both hands, start in the middle and spread the dough out with your palms while stretching the outer edges with your fingers. You should have an approximately 12 by 8 inch (30 x 20 cm) rectangle.

Lift up the edge farthest from yourself and slide your fingers under the dough. Move to the direct zone of your grill and place the bottom edge of the dough at the farthest point from you and pull the dough toward you to place on grill. Gently lift up 1 edge of the dough with the tongs to check for color. When you see some color setting in, lift the dough and give it a quarter turn with the peel. When the dough is sufficiently browned on the bottom, but not charred, remove it from the direct zone and flip it over onto the indirect zone.

Drizzle with olive oil and brush the crust evenly. Sprinkle Manchego onto the crust, add the chorizo and move to the direct side of the grill. Rotate the pizza every 15 to 30 seconds to crisp the bottom. When the bottom is crispy, remove the pizza from the grill, top with the kale and sprinkle the remaining 2 tablespoons (35 g) of Manchego over the top. Slice and serve.

CHORIZO, ROASTED CORN, COTIJA AND CREMA PIZZA

This pizza has all the flavors of a Mexican street taco. Typically you would see a chorizo taco combined with chunks of potatoes. I have substituted roasted corn to add a little bit more sweetness to the flavor combination. The Cotija and crema help bring the flavors together with some nice smooth creaminess. This will go great with a Michelada.

 YIELDS I PIZZA

INGREDIENTS

5 oz (142 g) oiled Pizza Dough ball (page 17)

Extra virgin olive oil

1 c (130 g) shredded Monterey Jack cheese

6 oz (170 g) chorizo, removed from casing, crumbled and caramelized in a sauté pan to fully cooked

1 ear of sweet corn, toasted on the grill and kernels removed and reserved

½ c (70 g) of Cotija cheese

10–12 very thin slices of jalapeño

2 tbsp (30 ml) Mexican crema (or substitute sour cream mixed with a little lime juice)

Cilantro leaves, for garnish

½ lime, cut into 4 wedges

DIRECTIONS

Lightly grease a metal work surface and the palms of your hands. Place the dough ball in the center of the surface and press down evenly with the palm of your hand. Working with both hands, start in the middle and spread the dough out with your palms while stretching the outer edges with your fingers. You should have an approximately 12 by 8 inch (30 x 20 cm) rectangle.

Lift up the edge farthest from yourself and slide your fingers under the dough. Move to the direct zone of your grill and place the bottom edge of the dough at the farthest point from you and pull the dough toward you to place on grill. Gently lift up 1 edge of the dough with the tongs to check for color. When you see some color setting in, lift the dough and give it a quarter turn with the peel. When the dough is sufficiently browned on the bottom, but not charred, remove it from the direct zone and flip it over onto the indirect zone.

Drizzle with olive oil and brush the crust evenly. Spread the Monterey Jack cheese all around the shell and distribute the chorizo and corn evenly. Move to the direct side of the grill and rotate every 15 to 30 seconds. Move the pizza to the indirect side of the grill and close the cover to make sure the top ingredients get heated through. When the cheese is melted and the top ingredients are hot, then sprinkle the Cotija and jalapeños around. Drizzle the crema and top with cilantro leaves for garnish. Place the limes around the outside edge so people can squeeze a little juice for brightness if they wish. Slice and serve.

BRUNCH AND DESSERT FAVORITES

Who of us hasn't gotten up in the morning and just reached for a leftover piece of pizza to start the day? These brunch pizzas certainly do not need to be limited to that festive midday party—feel free to have breakfast for dinner and dinner for breakfast in the case of the Weisswurst, Sauerkraut and Curry Ketchup Pizza. Toppings and combinations are endless and you should experiment. If it can go on toast, English muffins or in a pie or a dessert you pretty much have a brunch or dessert pizza in sight. Don't miss out on the Banana, Caramel and Cream Cheese Pizza. Those ingredients garnered a perfect score in the Jack Daniel's World Barbecue Championship dessert category.

RAMP, BACON AND EGG PIZZA

Joe Cassinelli, the owner of Pizzeria Posto (as well as a few other restaurants) is one hell of a chef and a very good friend. Joe and his pizzeria are certified by the Associazione Verace Pizza Napoletana in Naples, Italy. That means that he has to adhere to the very high standards and exact specifications of the association's rules for true Neapolitan-style pizza. The pizzas that come out of the wood-burning oven at Posto are spectacular with a beautifully charred crust. This is a grilled version of a pizza Joe ran as a special for brunch in the spring when ramps were in season. Cheese, bacon, ramps and an egg in the middle make for a very nice start to the day. Joe recommends serving this pizza with a crisp white. Try wines from the Soave zone in the Veneto.

➡ YIELDS I PIZZA

INGREDIENTS

1 large egg

5 oz (142 g) oiled Pizza Dough ball (page 17)

Extra virgin olive oil

3 oz (85 g) fresh Mozzarella, sliced thinly

¼ c (35 g) Asiago cheese, shredded

2 tbsp (17 g) grated Parmesan

4 slices smoked bacon, cooked and cut into ½-inch (13 mm) pieces

½ c (20 g) loosely packed ramp leaves, cut into ½-inch (13 mm) pieces

Flaky sea salt, for garnish

DIRECTIONS

Heat a small nonstick skillet over medium heat, crack the egg in the pan and cook until the whites begin to set. Flip the egg and remove from the heat. Just before the pizza comes off the grill, warm the egg on the medium-low side of the grill.

Clean the grill.

Lightly grease a metal work surface and the palms of your hands. Place the dough ball in the center of the surface and press down evenly with the palm of your hand. Working with both hands, start in the middle and spread the dough out with your palms while stretching the outer edges with your fingers. You should have an approximately 12 by 8 inch (30 x 20 cm) rectangle.

Lift up the edge farthest from yourself and slide your fingers under the dough. Move to the direct zone of your grill and place the bottom edge of the dough at the farthest point from you and pull the dough toward you to place on grill. Gently lift up 1 edge of the dough with the tongs to check for color. When you see some color setting in, lift the dough and give it a quarter turn with the peel. When the dough is sufficiently browned on the bottom, but not charred, remove it from the direct zone and flip it over onto the indirect zone.

Drizzle with olive oil and brush the crust evenly. Arrange the slices of Mozzarella all around the pizza, sprinkle on the Asiago and Parmesan. Add the bacon and ramp leaves. Move the pizza to the direct side of the grill and rotate every 15 to 30 seconds to crisp the bottom. When the bottom is crispy and the cheese is melted, remove from the grill, place the egg in the center, drizzle with olive oil and sprinkle a bit of salt around the pizza.

WEISSWURST, SAUERKRAUT AND CURRY KETCHUP PIZZA

My buddy Sal Fristensky is a New York City firefighter and a kick-ass chef in his own right. I hope the people in his station appreciate the food he makes. Sal came up to visit my wife Katy and me in Vermont and asked if there was something he could bring. The immediate answer was German sausages. He cooked up some cubed smoked bacon in a pan, added the sauerkraut and a touch of beer and then browned up the sausages and served it all on a platter with warm pretzels and curry ketchup. That was our breakfast. No need to ask what happened to the open beer. This is a version of that breakfast on a pizza. It's pretty hearty. You will have more sauerkraut than you need, which is never a bad thing.

➡️ YIELDS 1 PIZZA

INGREDIENTS

2 oz (57 g) good-quality smoked slab bacon, cut into ¼-inch (6 mm) cubes

4 oz (113 g) sauerkraut (from the refrigerated section)

4 oz (118 ml) good-quality lager style beer

4 oz (113 g) weisswurst (you can substitute bratwurst if you wish)

5 oz (142 g) oiled Pizza Dough ball (page 17)

Extra virgin olive oil

Curry ketchup (I like the Hela brand mild version.)

DIRECTIONS

Heat a skillet to medium-high heat and lightly brown the bacon, add the sauerkraut and beer and cook until almost all the liquid is gone. Remove from the pan and reserve. Measure out 1 cup (232 g) for the pizza and save the rest.

Weisswurst is already cooked but you should roll it around on the grill to caramelize the outside. When cool enough to handle, slice crosswise into thin pieces.

Clean the grill.

Lightly grease a metal work surface and the palms of your hands. Place the dough ball in the center of the surface and press down evenly with the palm of your hand. Working with both hands, start in the middle and spread the dough out with your palms while stretching the outer edges with your fingers. You should have an approximately 12 by 8 inch (30 x 20 cm) rectangle.

Lift up the edge farthest from yourself and slide your fingers under the dough. Move to the direct zone of your grill and place the bottom edge of the dough at the farthest point from you and pull the dough toward you to place on grill. Gently lift up 1 edge of the dough with the tongs to check for color. When you see some color setting in, lift the dough and give it a quarter turn with the peel. When the dough is sufficiently browned on the bottom, but not charred, remove it from the direct zone and flip it over onto the indirect zone.

Drizzle with olive oil and brush the crust. Squirt enough ketchup for a thin coating onto the crust and spread all over with the back of a spoon. Add the sauerkraut, scatter all of the sausage around the pizza and close the lid on the grill for 1 minute to heat up the toppings. Move the pizza to the direct side of the grill and rotate every 15 to 30 seconds until the bottom is crispy. Remove from the grill, squirt some more ketchup all over the pizza, slice and serve. Beer is optional if you are having this for breakfast.

BACON, ONION AND JARLSBERG PIZZA

This pizza is one of my favorites to break out on the morning of a grilling or barbecue competition. I usually make this on cold winter mornings to warm the house with the smell of smoky bacon and creamy melty cheesiness. It works just as well on the grill. Try cracking a farm fresh egg into a small nonstick skillet and place it off to the medium-low side of the grill. By the time your pizza is finished you can slide a perfectly cooked sunny-side up egg onto your pizza. Crack the yolk and you can dip your slices into it.

 **YIELDS 1 PIZZA**

INGREDIENTS

5 oz (142 g) oiled Pizza Dough ball (page 17)

Extra virgin olive oil

6 oz (170 g) Jarlsberg cheese, shredded (or good quality Swiss cheese)

5 strips smoked bacon, cooked and cut into 1 inch (2.5 cm) pieces

¼ c (35 g) thinly sliced red onion

1 sprig fresh thyme, leaves removed

Large pinch of thinly sliced flat-leaf parsley

Freshly cracked pepper

Sea salt

1 egg (optional)

DIRECTIONS

Lightly grease a metal work surface and the palms of your hands. Place the dough ball in the center of the surface and press down evenly with the palm of your hand. Working with both hands, start in the middle and spread the dough out with your palms while stretching the outer edges with your fingers. You should have an approximately 12 by 8 inch (30 x 20 cm) rectangle.

Lift up the edge farthest from yourself and slide your fingers under the dough. Move to the direct zone of your grill and place the bottom edge of the dough at the farthest point from you and pull the dough toward you to place on grill. Gently lift up 1 edge of the dough with the tongs to check for color. When you see some color setting in, lift the dough and give it a quarter turn with the peel. When the dough is sufficiently browned on the bottom, but not charred, remove it from the direct zone and flip it over onto the indirect zone.

Drizzle with olive oil and brush the crust evenly. Sprinkle on the Jarlsberg evenly, scatter the bacon all over the top and do the same with the red onion. Sprinkle the thyme, parsley and black pepper around and move to the direct side of the grill. Rotate the pizza every 15 to 30 seconds to crisp the bottom. Remove the pizza from the grill and drizzle some olive oil around and sprinkle a little bit of sea salt. Add the egg if you are using it, slice and serve.

SMOKED SALMON, CRÈME FRAÎCHE AND CAPER GRILLED PIZZA

This is a very simple grilled pizza that is great on a nice sunny day for brunch. If you want to really be a high roller add some Oscietra caviar and break out a big bottle of bubbly.

 YIELDS 1 PIZZA

INGREDIENTS

3 tbsp (44 ml) crème fraîche

1 tbsp (3 g) thinly sliced chives

5 oz (142 g) oiled Pizza Dough ball (page 17)

Extra virgin olive oil

2 oz (57 g) cream cheese at room temperature

4 oz (113 g) of thinly sliced smoked salmon

2 tbsp (17 g) capers, drained and rinsed

Chervil leaves, for garnish (optional)

DIRECTIONS

Put the crème fraîche in a small bowl and stir it a bit to loosen the texture. Add the chives and stir to combine.

Lightly grease a metal work surface and the palms of your hands. Place the dough ball in the center of the surface and press down evenly with the palm of your hand. Working with both hands, start in the middle and spread the dough out with your palms while stretching the outer edges with your fingers. You should have an approximately 12 by 8 inch (30 x 20 cm) rectangle.

Lift up the edge farthest from yourself and slide your fingers under the dough. Move to the direct zone of your grill and place the bottom edge of the dough at the farthest point from you and pull the dough toward you to place on grill. Gently lift up 1 edge of the dough with the tongs to check for color. When you see some color setting in, lift the dough and give it a quarter turn with the peel. When the dough is sufficiently browned on the bottom, but not charred, remove it from the direct zone and flip it over onto the indirect zone.

Drizzle with olive oil and brush the crust. Spread the cream cheese around with the back of a spoon. Arrange the salmon nicely around the pizza and sprinkle on the capers. Move the pizza to the direct side of the grill and rotate every 15 to 30 seconds, but try to get it as crisp as you want it as quickly as you can.

Remove the pizza from the grill, drizzle the chive–crème fraîche mixture all around and scatter the chervil leaves if you have chosen to use them. Slice and serve.

HAM, PEA, BÉCHAMEL AND TARRAGON PIZZA

Here is another pizza that is a loose translation of a pasta dish. The subtle earthy flavors of the peas are accentuated by the licorice herbaceousness of the tarragon with the ham bringing in the salty, briny backbone.

 YIELDS 1 PIZZA

INGREDIENTS

¼ c (60 ml) Béchamel Sauce (page 163)

5 oz (142 g) oiled Pizza Dough ball (page 17)

Extra virgin olive oil

¾ c (105 g) Pizza Cheese Blend (page 20)

2 oz (57 g) shaved cooked ham

¼ c (35 g) frozen peas, thawed and dried

¼ c (35 g) grated Parmesan

1 sprig fresh tarragon leaves, removed and snipped cleanly with scissors

DIRECTIONS

Warm the béchamel in a small pan.

Lightly grease a metal work surface and the palms of your hands. Place the dough ball in the center of the surface and press down evenly with the palm of your hand. Working with both hands, start in the middle and spread the dough out with your palms while stretching the outer edges with your fingers. You should have an approximately 12 by 8 inch (30 x 20 cm) rectangle.

Lift up the edge farthest from yourself and slide your fingers under the dough. Move to the direct zone of your grill and place the bottom edge of the dough at the farthest point from you and pull the dough toward you to place on grill. Gently lift up 1 edge of the dough with the tongs to check for color. When you see some color setting in, lift the dough and give it a quarter turn with the peel. When the dough is sufficiently browned on the bottom, but not charred, remove it from the direct zone and flip it over onto the indirect zone.

Drizzle with olive oil and brush the crust evenly. Sprinkle on the Pizza Cheese Blend, then scatter the ham and peas, drizzle the béchamel all around and move the pizza to the direct side of the grill. Continue rotating the pizza until you are just about at the desired crispness, and then move to the indirect side and cover the grill for a minute to make sure the toppings get hot. Move back to the direct side for final crisping if needed and then remove from the grill. Sprinkle with the Parmesan and tarragon leaves and then drizzle just a little more olive oil around. Slice and serve.

BÉCHAMEL SAUCE

➡ YIELDS 1 ¼ CUPS (300 ML)

INGREDIENTS

2 oz (57 g) unsalted butter

2 oz (57 g) all purpose flour

1 c (240 ml) whole milk

DIRECTIONS

Heat the butter in a small saucepan, when melted add the flour and cook for 2 or 3 minutes, whisk in the milk in 3 batches to avoid lumps and continue stirring until the sauce comes to a boil. Reduce heat and whisk for another 30 seconds. Drain into a bowl and reserve.

STRAWBERRY AND NUTELLA PIZZA

Chris Hart, the pitmaster of the World Champion BBQ team iQue, was invited to be on a Food Network television show and I was fortunate enough to have him ask me to be his assistant. One of the ingredients in one of the challenges was pizza dough. We had a refrigerator and pantry of other things to choose from and I grabbed some strawberries and chocolate and made a dessert pizza. When I saw the episode on air, one of the judges made a mockery out of it with almost 3 Stooges–like flair. I know the pizza wasn't bad, and I'm guessing he did it for comedic effect. I did learn something from that though, and that is to put the strawberries on cut-side down so they won't fall off the pizza as you try to eat it. This is a version of that pizza I made for the show.

 YIELDS 1 PIZZA

INGREDIENTS

12 medium-size ripe strawberries, cut in half lengthwise

1 tbsp (12 g) granulated sugar

5 oz (142 g) oiled Pizza Dough ball (page 17)

½ c (120 ml) Nutella spread

Powdered sugar, for garnish

DIRECTIONS

Place the strawberries and granulated sugar in a bowl, mix to incorporate and let sit for 30 minutes.

Lightly grease a metal work surface and the palms of your hands. Place the dough ball in the center of the surface and press down evenly with the palm of your hand. Working with both hands, start in the middle and spread the dough out with your palms while stretching the outer edges with your fingers. You should have an approximately 12 by 8 inch (30 x 20 cm) rectangle.

Lift up the edge farthest from yourself and slide your fingers under the dough. Move to the direct zone of your grill and place the bottom edge of the dough at the farthest point from you and pull the dough toward you to place on grill. Gently lift up 1 edge of the dough with the tongs to check for color. When you see some color setting in, lift the dough and give it a quarter turn with the peel. When the dough is sufficiently browned on the bottom, but not charred, remove it from the direct zone and flip it over onto the indirect zone.

When you turn over the pizza onto the indirect side of the grill, spread the Nutella all over with the back of a spoon. Place the strawberries on the pizza cut-side down in a checkerboard pattern. Move the pizza to the direct side of the grill and rotate every 15 to 30 seconds to crisp the bottom. When the bottom is crispy, remove from the grill, dust with the powdered sugar, slice and serve.

BLUEBERRY AND RICOTTA PIZZA

Blueberries are in season in New England from around the middle of June to around the end of August. This is a simple pizza, so depending on what type of blueberries you like may help you decide what part of the season you may want to make this pizza (assuming you are using local berries). The early season tends to produce small tart berries. Too late in the season and I think the blueberries lose some of their unique flavor. I am more of a three-quarters-into-the-season blueberry person where hopefully I am getting blueberries that have a sufficient amount of rain and plenty of sunshine and are bursting with great flavor. Use whichever you prefer. This pizza goes great with a glass of ice-cold milk.

→ YIELDS I PIZZA

INGREDIENTS

5 oz (142 g) oiled Pizza Dough ball (page 17)

Extra virgin olive oil

Powdered sugar

1 c (250 g) Ricotta cheese

1 c (148 g) fresh blueberries

DIRECTIONS

Lightly grease a metal work surface and the palms of your hands. Place the dough ball in the center of the surface and press down evenly with the palm of your hand. Working with both hands, start in the middle and spread the dough out with your palms while stretching the outer edges with your fingers. You should have an approximately 12 by 8 inch (30 x 20 cm) rectangle.

Lift up the edge farthest from yourself and slide your fingers under the dough. Move to the direct zone of your grill and place the bottom edge of the dough at the farthest point from you and pull the dough toward you to place on grill. Gently lift up 1 edge of the dough with the tongs to check for color. When you see some color setting in, lift the dough and give it a quarter turn with the peel. When the dough is sufficiently browned on the bottom, but not charred, remove it from the direct zone and flip it over onto the indirect zone.

Drizzle with olive oil and brush the crust. Yep, we are using oil with this one. Sprinkle the crust with the powdered sugar. Add the ricotta and spread all over the dough, sprinkle the blueberries all around the pizza and close the lid on the grill for 1 to 2 minutes, checking the crust periodically to see if it needs to be moved to prevent burning. When the blueberries are hot, move the pizza to the direct side of the grill and rotate the crust every 15 to 30 seconds until the bottom is crispy. This will probably take a little less time than usual if the pizza was beginning to get crispy on the indirect side of the grill. Remove the pizza, sprinkle with powdered sugar, slice and serve.

BANANA, CARAMEL AND CREAM CHEESE PIZZA

This is a version of a dessert that got a perfect score at the Jack Daniel's World Invitational BBQ Championship in Lynchburg in 2009. That was the year our iQue team won the contest to become world champions. It was the first time any team from New England had won the contest. To say I was proud to be up on that stage with pitmaster Chris and his brother Jamie is quite an understatement. I chose to honor getting the perfect score by putting the dessert on the menu at our restaurant.

➡ YIELDS I PIZZA

INGREDIENTS

1 firm ripe banana, peeled and cut into ¼-inch (6 mm) cubes

1 tbsp (15 ml) Jack Daniel's (you can omit this if you need to)

½ c (120 ml) caramel sauce

5 oz (142 g) oiled Pizza Dough ball (page 17)

4 oz (113) cream cheese, softened at room temperature

2 tbsp (8 g) graham cracker crumbs

DIRECTIONS

Place the banana, Jack Daniel's and the caramel sauce in a bowl and toss to combine.

Lightly grease a metal work surface and the palms of your hands. Place the dough ball in the center of the surface and press down evenly with the palm of your hand. Working with both hands, start in the middle and spread the dough out with your palms while stretching the outer edges with your fingers. You should have an approximately 12 by 8 inch (30 x 20 cm) rectangle.

Lift up the edge farthest from yourself and slide your fingers under the dough. Move to the direct zone of your grill and place the bottom edge of the dough at the farthest point from you and pull the dough toward you to place on grill. Gently lift up 1 edge of the dough with the tongs to check for color. When you see some color setting in, lift the dough and give it a quarter turn with the peel. When the dough is sufficiently browned on the bottom, but not charred, remove it from the direct zone and flip it over onto the indirect zone.

When you turn over the pizza onto the indirect side of the grill add the cream cheese and spread all over evenly. Spoon dollops of the banana mixture all around the pizza. Move the pizza to the hot side of the grill and rotate every 15 to 30 seconds until the bottom is crispy. Remove the pizza from the grill, sprinkle with crumbs, slice and serve.

INDEPENDENCE DAY PIZZA

Katy and I were staying over at her mom Pat's house for a family wedding during the time I was writing this book. It was a fairly stressful time as we had just closed our restaurant in Essex Junction and the cookbook deadline was looming. Pat, an avid writer, was concerned that I wasn't close enough to finishing the book in time. She sprang out of bed the morning of the rehearsal dinner and said she was dreaming of pizzas for the book. She threw four ideas out at me rapid fire, and this is one of them. Happy Birthday, USA!

 YIELDS 1 PIZZA

INGREDIENTS

12 medium strawberries, hulled and cut in half lengthwise

1 tbsp (12 g) granulated sugar

1 tbsp (15 ml) orange liqueur such as Cointreau or Triple Sec

5 oz (142 g) oiled Pizza Dough ball (page 17)

⅓ c (86 g) blueberry preserves

Good-quality canned whipped cream

DIRECTIONS

Place the strawberries, sugar and orange liqueur in a bowl and stir to incorporate. Let sit for 30 minutes.

Lightly grease a metal work surface and the palms of your hands. Place the dough ball in the center of the surface and press down evenly with the palm of your hand. Working with both hands, start in the middle and spread the dough out with your palms while stretching the outer edges with your fingers. You should have an approximately 12 by 8 inch (30 x 20 cm) rectangle.

Lift up the edge farthest from yourself and slide your fingers under the dough. Move to the direct zone of your grill and place the bottom edge of the dough at the farthest point from you and pull the dough toward you to place on grill. Gently lift up 1 edge of the dough with the tongs to check for color. When you see some color setting in, lift the dough and give it a quarter turn with the peel. When the dough is sufficiently browned on the bottom, but not charred, remove it from the direct zone and flip it over onto the indirect zone.

When you turn over the pizza onto the indirect side of the grill, spread the blueberry preserves all over with the back of a spoon. Place the strawberries all around the pizza in a checkerboard-type pattern. Move the pizza to the direct side of the grill and rotate every 15 to 30 seconds until the bottom is crispy. When the bottom is crispy, remove the pizza from the grill and spray the whipped cream in little dots all over the pizza (kind of like stars), slice and serve.

FLATBREADS

At their simplest, flatbreads are merely composed of water, flour and salt. Sometimes a leavening agent is used such as yeast. I use my regular pizza dough recipe in the following recipes just for consistency. There are a couple of recipes that are a little different, such as the Cheese and Smoked Bacon Fougasse where we take the dough and roll bacon and cheese into it. The 647's Grilled Flatbread With Curried Gremolata uses an entirely different dough and technique. I encourage you to try different dough combinations or add-ins and toppings as you explore and develop your pizza and flatbread grilling repertoire. Some of the flatbreads here could be complete meals such as the Grilled Halibut, Avocado and Roasted Tomato Salsa Flatbread and the Gyro Grilled Flatbread. Others are meant as accompaniments, such as the Carta Musica and the Aglio, Olio and Pepperoncino. Don't miss out on the simple brilliance of the Prosciutto and Parmigiano Reggiano Flatbread or the Pan con Tomate, both with transformative powers. Be creative and use flavors that are both familiar and unfamiliar—there really isn't much to lose but plenty to gain. Just remember to have fun.

CHEESE AND SMOKED BACON FOUGASSE

This flatbread was inspired by trips to the south of France. Fougasse is a great snack to have on hand. The technique here is a little different and the size of the dough is a little larger than most of the pizzas listed in this book. The fougasse is a little thicker than the grilled pizza because we are going to actually incorporate the ingredients into the dough. It's an extra step but one you will find worth doing.

 YIELDS 2 FLATBREADS

INGREDIENTS

16 oz (454 g) Pizza Dough, divided in half (page 17)

6 slices of smoked bacon, cooked (not too crispy) and cut into ¼-inch (6 mm) strips crosswise

1 c (140 g) shredded Cheddar cheese

Extra virgin olive oil

Flour for dusting if needed

DIRECTIONS

Place 1 of the dough pieces on a clean surface and spread the dough out into a 6-inch (15 cm) circle, add half the bacon and half the cheese to the dough and start folding in from the outside to the middle (if the dough sticks, then lightly dust the surface with flour). Repeat this process a couple of times to distribute the bacon and cheese evenly throughout the dough. Roll the dough into a ball and place on a lightly floured surface for about 5 minutes. Repeat with the other piece of dough. If you want to make a large batch of fougasse, it would probably be easier to incorporate the cheese and the bacon in a stand mixer with the dough hook during the middle of the kneading process.

Oil a cookie sheet with just enough olive oil to coat the 2 dough balls. Roll the balls in the oil and let rest to proof for a bit.

Lightly grease a metal work surface and the palms of your hands. Place the dough ball in the center of the surface and press down evenly with the palm of your hand. Working with both hands, start in the middle and spread the dough out with your palms while stretching the outer edges with your fingers. Press it out to between ¼ and ⅓ of an inch (6 to 8 mm) (thicker than the pizza shells).

Lift up the edge farthest from yourself and slide your fingers under the dough. Move to the direct zone of your grill and place the bottom edge of the dough at the farthest point from you and pull the dough toward you to place on grill. Gently lift up 1 edge of the dough with the tongs to check for color. When you see some color setting in, lift the dough and give it a quarter turn with the peel. When the dough is sufficiently browned on the bottom, but not charred, remove it from the direct zone and flip it over onto the indirect zone.

Drizzle with olive oil and brush the crust evenly. Move to the direct side of the grill and rotate continually to crisp the bottom but not as crisp as a normal flatbread. When the bottom is slightly crispy move the fougasse to the indirect side of the grill and close the lid for 1 minute or 2 to finish cooking the dough. Check a few times to make sure the bottom does not burn. Brush with a little more olive oil and remove from the grill. Serve whole to allow people to tear apart their own pieces. Breaking bread has never been so tasty.

GRILLED HALIBUT, AVOCADO AND ROASTED TOMATO SALSA FLATBREAD

This flatbread is inspired by a taco served at my good friend and James Beard award–winning chef Ken Oringer's sashimi bar Uni, inside his world-famous restaurant Clio at the Eliot Hotel. Ken and I have spent countless hours together behind the sashimi bar serving guests and the grilled halibut tacos were ordered by almost every table. Yes, we did serve cooked fish at the sashimi bar! The yuzu kosho lends an almost fermented-like spicy sourness that is a spectacular and shining flavor component in the flatbread. I think it is worth seeking out for the recipe. Our favorite sake, Daishichi Kimoto Honjozo, is an excellent drink pairing.

 **YIELDS I FLATBREAD**

INGREDIENTS

6 oz (170 g) boneless and skinless halibut fillet (about ½-inch [13 mm] thick tail portion is ideal)

1 tbsp (15 ml) blended oil

Salt

Freshly ground black pepper

1 tbsp (15 ml) yuzu kosho

2 tbsp (30 ml) low-sodium soy sauce

¼ c (35 g) sweet onion, finely diced

1 tsp (5 g) espelette pepper (or ½ tsp each of cayenne and sweet smoked paprika)

2 tbsp (30 ml) extra virgin olive oil, plus more for the flatbread

1 tbsp (15 ml) fresh-squeezed lemon juice

2 tbsp (6 g) thinly sliced scallion (green part only)

5 oz (142 g) oiled Pizza Dough ball (page 17)

2 tbsp (30 ml) Avocado Crema (page 175)

2 tbsp (30 ml) Salsa Ranchera (page 151)

2 tbsp (30 ml) Pickled Jalapeño Crema (page 175)

Cilantro leaves, for garnish

DIRECTIONS

Rub the halibut with the blended oil and season with salt and pepper. Place the halibut over a medium-heat fire on the grill and cook for 2 minutes, rotate the halibut 90 degrees and cook for another 2 minutes, flip the halibut and cook for 2 minutes longer. Remove the halibut from the grill and place in a bowl. When the halibut has cooled slightly and can be handled, flake it in the bowl. Add the yuzu kosho, soy sauce, onion, espelette pepper, olive oil, lemon juice and scallion to the bowl. Toss all the ingredients to combine and place aside.

Brush and clean the grill.

Lightly grease a metal work surface and the palms of your hands. Place the dough ball in the center of the surface and press down evenly with the palm of your hand. Working with both hands, start in the middle and spread the dough out with your palms while stretching the outer edges with your fingers. You should have an approximately 12 by 8 inch (30 x 20 cm) rectangle.

Lift up the edge farthest from yourself and slide your fingers under the dough. Move to the direct zone of your grill and place the bottom edge of the dough at the farthest point from you and pull the dough toward you to place on grill. Gently lift up 1 edge of the dough with the tongs to check for color. When you see some color setting in, lift the dough and give it a quarter turn with the peel. When the dough is sufficiently browned on the bottom, but not charred, remove it from the direct zone and flip it over onto the indirect zone.

When you turn over the flatbread onto the indirect side of the grill, brush the flatbread with olive oil. Sprinkle the halibut mixture all over the flatbread. Move the flatbread to the direct side of the grill and rotate every 15 to 30 seconds to crisp the bottom. When the bottom is crispy remove from the grill, drizzle the Avocado Crema, Salsa Ranchera and Jalapeño Crema all over the flatbread, scatter the cilantro all over, slice and serve.

AVOCADO CREMA

➡ YIELDS JUST LESS THAN 1 CUP (240 ML)

INGREDIENTS

½ c (115 g) ripe avocado

¼ c (120 ml) sour cream

2 tbsp (30 ml) fresh-squeezed lime juice

1 tsp (5 g) salt

DIRECTIONS

Place all ingredients in a blender and blend on high. Transfer to a covered container and refrigerate until needed. The Avocado Crema will keep in the refrigerator for 3 days.

PICKLED JALAPEÑO CREMA

➡ YIELDS ¾ CUP (180 ML)

INGREDIENTS

½ c (120 ml) sour cream

2 tbsp (17 g) diced, canned pickled jalapeño

1 tbsp (15 ml) pickled jalapeño juice

DIRECTIONS

Place all ingredients in a blender and blend on high. Transfer to a covered container and refrigerate until needed. The Pickled Jalapeño Crema will keep in the refrigerator for 7 days.

LOMI LOMI SALMON FLATBREAD

Lomi Lomi Salmon is a traditional Hawaiian side dish. It is usually made with salted salmon that needs to be soaked in water overnight. The salmon is then tossed by hand (the word lomi is Hawaiian for massage) with fresh tomatoes and sweet onions. It is a vibrant and refreshing side dish. I like to use fresh salmon and grill it to medium rare before tearing it into pieces and mixing with the tomatoes. This is one of those healthier flatbreads that still brings some great flavor to the table.

➡ YIELDS I FLATBREAD

INGREDIENTS

4 oz (113 g) salmon fillet (from the head end is preferable), skinned and pin bones removed

Extra virgin olive oil

Salt

Freshly ground black pepper

4 oz (113 g) Ricotta cheese

1 tbsp (3 g) thinly sliced chives, plus more for garnish

1 tbsp (15 ml) crème fraîche or sour cream

12 grape tomatoes, cut in half lengthwise

¼ c (35 g) thinly sliced sweet onion cut across the grain

1 tbsp (15 ml) cider vinegar

5 oz (142 g) oiled Pizza Dough ball (page 17)

DIRECTIONS

Rub the salmon fillet all over lightly with oil and season with salt and pepper. Place the fillet over a medium-high heat fire on the grill. Cook for 2 to 3 minutes, flip and cook for 2 more minutes. You want the salmon to be rare to medium rare. If you prefer your salmon more well-done, then just cook it a little longer. Set the salmon aside to cool.

Clean the grill.

Combine the ricotta, 1 tablespoon (3 g) chives and crème fraîche in a small bowl and stir to combine. Reserve.

When the salmon is cool enough to handle, tear into bite-size pieces. Place the salmon, tomatoes, onion and cider vinegar in a bowl. Season with salt and pepper and toss the mixture with your hands or gently with a spoon.

Lightly grease a metal work surface and the palms of your hands. Place the dough ball in the center of the surface and press down evenly with the palm of your hand. Working with both hands, start in the middle and spread the dough out with your palms while stretching the outer edges with your fingers. You should have an approximately 12 by 8 inch (30 x 20 cm) rectangle.

Lift up the edge farthest from yourself and slide your fingers under the dough. Move to the direct zone of your grill and place the bottom edge of the dough at the farthest point from you and pull the dough toward you to place on grill. Gently lift up 1 edge of the dough with the tongs to check for color. When you see some color setting in, lift the dough and give it a quarter turn with the peel. When the dough is sufficiently browned on the bottom, but not charred, remove it from the direct zone and flip it over onto the indirect zone.

Drizzle with olive oil and brush the crust evenly. Move the flatbread to the direct side of the grill and rotate every 15 to 30 seconds to crisp the bottom. When the bottom is almost as crispy as you would like, add the Ricotta mixture and spread all over the flatbread with the back of a spoon. Add the salmon mixture to cover the flatbread, drizzle with olive oil, garnish with chives, slice and serve.

LAHMAJUN

Lahmajun is often referred to as the pizza of Armenia and the Middle East without all the fattening ingredients. If you can't find ground lamb, then substitute 90 percent lean ground beef. I think the sliced cornichon and lemon juice are essential ingredients in this flatbread.

 YIELDS 1 FLATBREAD

INGREDIENTS

2 tbsp (30 ml) olive oil, plus extra for the flatbread

1 clove garlic, finely diced

¼ c (35 g) yellow onion, finely dice

5 oz (142 g) lean ground lamb

1 tsp (2g) sweet paprika

½ c (120 ml) Basic Tomato Sauce (page 21)

1 tbsp (3 g) thinly slice flat-leaf parsley, plus more for garnish

Salt

Freshly ground black pepper

5 oz (142 g) oiled Pizza Dough ball (page 17)

8 cornichons, sliced into thirds lengthwise

1 tbsp (15 ml) fresh squeezed lemon juice

DIRECTIONS

In a medium sauté pan heat the 2 tablespoons (30 ml) of olive oil over medium heat, add the garlic and onion and cook until softened. Add the lamb and paprika and cook until lightly browned. Add the tomato sauce, 1 tablespoon (3 g) of parsley and cook until most of the moisture is gone (about 5 minutes). Season with salt and pepper and reserve in a bowl.

Lightly grease a metal work surface and the palms of your hands. Place the dough ball in the center of the surface and press down evenly with the palm of your hand. Working with both hands, start in the middle and spread the dough out with your palms while stretching the outer edges with your fingers. You should have an approximately 12 by 8 inch (30 x 20 cm) rectangle.

Lift up the edge farthest from yourself and slide your fingers under the dough. Move to the direct zone of your grill and place the bottom edge of the dough at the farthest point from you and pull the dough toward you to place on grill. Gently lift up 1 edge of the dough with the tongs to check for color. When you see some color setting in, lift the dough and give it a quarter turn with the peel. When the dough is sufficiently browned on the bottom, but not charred, remove it from the direct zone and flip it over onto the indirect zone.

Drizzle with olive oil and brush the crust. Spread the lamb and tomato mixture all over and move to the direct side of the grill. Rotate every 15 to 30 seconds until the bottom of the flatbread is crispy. Remove from the grill, scatter the cornichon, sprinkle the lemon juice and garnish with parsley. Slice and serve.

GYRO GRILLED FLATBREAD

Traditionally a gyro is a Greek rolled pita sandwich filled with roasted lamb, onions, tomatoes and tzatziki sauce, ingredients that lend themselves perfectly to a flatbread. I add some harissa paste (found in many middle eastern markets) for a little extra zip.

 YIELDS I FLATBREAD

INGREDIENTS

5 oz (142 g) lean lamb top round, trimmed of all fat and sinew

Salt

Freshly ground black pepper

2 tsp (10 g) dried Greek oregano

5 oz (142 g) oiled Pizza Dough ball (page 17)

Extra virgin olive oil

2 tbsp (17 g) harissa paste

1 ripe Roma tomato, chopped and seasoned with salt and pepper

½ small red onion, thinly sliced across the grain

Tzatziki Sauce (page 179)

1 tbsp (3 g) thinly sliced fresh mint

DIRECTIONS

Season the lamb with salt and pepper and cook over a medium-high heat fire, turning constantly until rare to medium rare (125°F [52°C]), about 5 to 7 minutes. Remove to a plate, sprinkle all over with the oregano and let it rest for about 5 minutes. Slice the lamb across the grain diagonally and set aside.

Clean the grill.

Lightly grease a metal work surface and the palms of your hands. Place the dough ball in the center of the surface and press down evenly with the palm of your hand. Working with both hands, start in the middle and spread the dough out with your palms while stretching the outer edges with your fingers. You should have an approximately 12 by 8 inch (30 x 20 cm) rectangle.

Lift up the edge farthest from yourself and slide your fingers under the dough. Move to the direct zone of your grill and place the bottom edge of the dough at the farthest point from you and pull the dough toward you to place on grill. Gently lift up 1 edge of the dough with the tongs to check for color. When you see some color setting in, lift the dough and give it a quarter turn with the peel. When the dough is sufficiently browned on the bottom, but not charred, remove it from the direct zone and flip it over onto the indirect zone.

Drizzle with olive oil and brush the crust. Spread the harissa paste all over the flatbread evenly with the back of a spoon. Place slices of the lamb all over, scatter the chopped tomato and onion and move the flatbread to the direct side of the grill. Rotate the flatbread every 15 to 30 seconds to crisp the bottom. When the bottom is crispy, remove from the grill, spoon dollops of the tzatziki sauce all over, sprinkle the mint and drizzle with olive oil, slice and serve.

TZATZIKI SAUCE

INGREDIENTS

½ c (120 ml) plain Greek-style yogurt

1 tbsp (17 g) minced, seeded cucumber

2 tsp (6 g) thinly sliced fresh mint

1 clove garlic, minced

1 tsp (5 ml) extra virgin olive oil

2 tsp (10 ml) fresh lemon juice

Salt

Freshly ground black pepper

DIRECTIONS

Add the yogurt, cucumber, mint, garlic, olive oil and lemon juice to a bowl and stir to combine. Season to taste with salt and freshly ground black pepper. Refrigerate until ready to use.

FIG JAM, GORGONZOLA AND PROSCIUTTO FLATBREAD

Fig jam is an amazing condiment. It is at once earthy, sweet and slightly acidic. Figs, stuffed with Gorgonzola, wrapped in prosciutto and roasted in the wood oven always sold very well when I was the chef at La Campania in Waltham, MA. We would drizzle a little aged balsamic over the top of them when they came out of the oven. Each bite was a little umami bomb. Here is a grilled flatbread version of those figs using a condiment you can have on hand all year round.

➡ YIELDS 1 FLATBREAD

INGREDIENTS

5 oz (142 g) oiled Pizza Dough ball (page 17)

Extra virgin olive oil

⅓ c (43 g) fig jam (Dalmatia brand is a very good one.)

¼ c (35 g) Gorgonzola, crumbled

4–5 thinly sliced pieces of prosciutto

DIRECTIONS

Lightly grease a metal work surface and the palms of your hands. Place the dough ball in the center of the surface and press down evenly with the palm of your hand. Working with both hands, start in the middle and spread the dough out with your palms while stretching the outer edges with your fingers. You should have an approximately 12 by 8 inch (30 x 20 cm) rectangle.

Lift up the edge farthest from yourself and slide your fingers under the dough. Move to the direct zone of your grill and place the bottom edge of the dough at the farthest point from you and pull the dough toward you to place on grill. Gently lift up 1 edge of the dough with the tongs to check for color. When you see some color setting in, lift the dough and give it a quarter turn with the peel. When the dough is sufficiently browned on the bottom, but not charred, remove it from the direct zone and flip it over onto the indirect zone.

Drizzle with olive oil and brush the crust evenly. Spread the jam all over the crust and sprinkle the Gorgonzola around the crust. Move the flatbread to the direct side of the grill and rotate every 15 to 30 seconds to crisp the bottom. When the bottom is crispy, remove from the grill, arrange the slices of prosciutto on the top, drizzle with olive oil, slice and serve.

PAN CON TOMATE FLATBREAD

This flatbread is inspired by the famous tapas dish Pan con Tomate—literally bread with tomato. It is super simple but requires very good ingredients and a ripe tomato. It can be eaten as is but sometimes is topped with thin sliced meats, cheese or as I prefer mine, with white anchovies.

 YIELDS 1 FLATBREAD

INGREDIENTS

1 medium to large ripe tomato

5 oz (142 g) oiled Pizza Dough ball (page 17)

Extra virgin olive oil, preferably a Spanish one

1 clove of garlic, grated on a microplane

Flaky sea salt (such as Maldon)

DIRECTIONS

Cut the tomato in half widthwise and grate it on a box grater over a bowl. Discard the skin.

Lightly grease a metal work surface and the palms of your hands. Place the dough ball in the center of the surface and press down evenly with the palm of your hand. Working with both hands, start in the middle and spread the dough out with your palms while stretching the outer edges with your fingers. You should have an approximately 12 by 8 inch (30 x 20 cm) rectangle.

Lift up the edge farthest from yourself and slide your fingers under the dough. Move to the direct zone of your grill and place the bottom edge of the dough at the farthest point from you and pull the dough toward you to place on grill. Gently lift up 1 edge of the dough with the tongs to check for color. When you see some color setting in, lift the dough and give it a quarter turn with the peel. When the dough is sufficiently browned on the bottom, but not charred, remove it from the direct zone and flip it over onto the indirect zone.

Drizzle with olive oil and brush the crust, spread the garlic all over the crust with a back of a spoon, add the tomato and spread evenly over the flatbread with the back of a spoon. Move the flatbread to the direct side of the grill and rotate every 15 to 30 seconds to crisp the bottom. When the bottom is crispy, remove the flatbread from the grill, drizzle with olive oil and sprinkle some salt all around, slice and serve.

CHEESY GARLIC FLATBREAD

This flatbread is basically garlic bread gone wild. It's great for snacking on, too, so make a few extras for later in the day or to serve with a favorite pasta dish.

➡ YIELDS | FLATBREAD

INGREDIENTS

1 tsp (2 g) unsalted butter

2 tbsp (30 ml) extra virgin olive oil

2 cloves garlic, peeled and sliced thinly

5 oz (142 g) oiled Pizza Dough ball (page 17)

¾ c (105 g) grated Asiago cheese

2 tbsp (17 g) grated Pecorino Romano

Freshly ground black pepper

Thinly sliced chives, for garnish

DIRECTIONS

Heat a skillet over medium heat and add the butter and olive oil. When the butter melts, add all of the garlic and cook until the garlic turns a light golden color, for about 5 minutes, remove from the pan, strain the garlic and reserve both the garlic and infused oil/butter separately.

Lightly grease a metal work surface and the palms of your hands. Place the dough ball in the center of the surface and press down evenly with the palm of your hand. Working with both hands, start in the middle and spread the dough out with your palms while stretching the outer edges with your fingers. You should have an approximately 12 by 8 inch (30 x 20 cm) rectangle.

Lift up the edge farthest from yourself and slide your fingers under the dough. Move to the direct zone of your grill and place the bottom edge of the dough at the farthest point from you and pull the dough toward you to place on grill. Gently lift up 1 edge of the dough with the tongs to check for color. When you see some color setting in, lift the dough and give it a quarter turn with the peel. When the dough is sufficiently browned on the bottom, but not charred, remove it from the direct zone and flip it over onto the indirect zone.

When you turn over the flatbread onto the indirect side of the grill, drizzle with a little of the garlic-infused oil/butter and brush the crust. Sprinkle the Asiago and Romano all over the flatbread. Scatter the garlic all over and sprinkle with pepper. Move the flatbread to the direct side of the grill and rotate every 15 to 30 seconds to crisp the bottom. When the bottom is crispy, remove from the grill, drizzle 1 tablespoon (15 ml) of the infused oil around the flatbread, sprinkle with chives and serve. If you are making extras for later, cool the flatbreads on a rack so they don't get too soggy.

647'S GRILLED FLATBREAD WITH CURRY GREMOLATA

Tremont 647 in Boston's South End is owned and operated by my good friend, barbecue teammate and chef Andy Husbands. Andy is a big proponent of live-fire cooking and big bold flavors that he features in his adventurous American cuisine. I met Andy in 1996 when we were both opening restaurants and we would meet after work and have drinks. Andy invited me to join the iQue competition barbecue team at the American Royal in 2006, and we have been cooking together ever since. The two of us represented iQue in the "I Know Jack About Grillin'!" contest at the 2011 Jack Daniel's World Barbecue Championship. This proved to be yet another very proud moment in my cooking career as Andy and I ended up taking top honors in the grilling contest. Andy likes to refer to us as "Barbecue Gangstas" and I hope the gangstas are lucky enough to get together and try to win it again.

➜ YIELDS 8 (8-INCH [20 CM]) FLATBREADS

INGREDIENTS

1 tsp (3 g) dried yeast
½ c (120 ml) warm water
½ c (120 ml) warm milk
1 tsp (4 g) brown sugar
1½ c (192 g) all purpose flour
½ c (64 g) whole wheat flour
¼ tsp baking powder
½ tsp kosher salt
4 tbsp (60 ml) plain yogurt
2 tbsp (28 g) butter, melted
Butter, for the proofing process
Extra virgin olive oil, for grilling
Curry Gremolata Butter (page 185)

DIRECTIONS

Place the yeast, water, milk in a small mixer with a dough hook, mix for 20 seconds and then let sit for 5 minutes to become frothy. In a separate bowl, mix together the brown sugar, flours, baking powder and salt. Sift.

Once the yeast mixture has become frothy, add the yogurt and melted butter and mix on low for 1 minute. Add the sifted flour mixture and mix on low for 1 minute, then increase speed to medium for 3 to 4 minutes until the dough is elastic.

Remove from bowl, place on a lightly floured surface and knead for 30 seconds. Make into ball and place in buttered bowl, cover tight with plastic wrap and let proof/rise in a warm place for 2 to 3 hours until doubled in size.

Grill lightly so it will have an even, low temperature.

Remove dough from the bowl and separate into 8 even pieces. Roll into balls and cover with a damp cloth and let rise for 30 minutes more.

While dough is proofing for the second time, make Gremolata.

Roll balls out into ¼ inch (6 mm)-thick discs. Lightly oil each one and grill 1 or 2 at a time over low heat until golden brown, about 2 to 3 minutes, flip over and repeat process. When the bread is done, slather with Curry Gremolata Butter, cut into wedges and serve immediately.

CURRY GREMOLATA BUTTER

➡ YIELDS ³/₄ CUP (180 G)

INGREDIENTS

4 oz (113 g) butter, salted, at room temperature

1 tbsp (18 g) sea salt (I use Maldon.)

1 tbsp (6 g) curry powder

½ c (8 g) cilantro leaves, roughly chopped

2 limes, zest only, minced

2 garlic cloves, minced

DIRECTIONS

Mix all ingredients until fully incorporated. Store in the fridge for up to 2 weeks.

LA TUR AND WILDFLOWER HONEY FLATBREAD

La Tur is an earthy-flavored cheese with a lingering tang made from cow, goat and sheep milk. The first time I had it was as a cheese course in a restaurant in Miami. Spectacularly unctuous, it seemed to be melting from the outside in. It was simply paired with some local honey and a toasted baguette. I have been in love with La Tur ever since. It goes very well with Asti Spumante.

 YIELDS | FLATBREAD

INGREDIENTS

5 oz (142 g) oiled Pizza Dough ball
(page 17)

Extra virgin olive oil

3 oz (85 g) ripe La Tur (half wheel)

Wildflower honey

DIRECTIONS

Lightly grease a metal work surface and the palms of your hands. Place the dough ball in the center of the surface and press down evenly with the palm of your hand. Working with both hands, start in the middle and spread the dough out with your palms while stretching the outer edges with your fingers. You should have an approximately 12 by 8 inch (30 x 20 cm) rectangle.

Lift up the edge farthest from yourself and slide your fingers under the dough. Move to the direct zone of your grill and place the bottom edge of the dough at the farthest point from you and pull the dough toward you to place on grill. Gently lift up 1 edge of the dough with the tongs to check for color. When you see some color setting in, lift the dough and give it a quarter turn with the peel. When the dough is sufficiently browned on the bottom, but not charred, remove it from the direct zone and flip it over onto the indirect zone.

Drizzle with olive oil and brush the crust. Move the crust to the direct side of the grill and begin to crisp the bottom, rotating every 15 to 30 seconds. When the crust is almost as crispy as you would like, move it to the indirect side of the grill and keep the pizza peel underneath it. Spread the La Tur all over the flatbread and drizzle a good amount of honey over it (as much as you like). Slice into squares and serve.

PROSCIUTTO AND PARMIGIANO REGGIANO FLATBREAD

This is one of those very few ingredient flatbreads that really requires superior ingredients to shine. It is very simple and yet very satisfying. It is also umami rich from the Parmigiano and very addictive. I really enjoy prosciutto from around the region of Langhirano. It's probably from fond memories of driving through the region and smelling curing prosciutto in the air. Try to find a light olive oil from Liguria made from Taggiasca olives, which will not overpower the prosciutto and will have a slightly peppery finish. I like to drink this with a light white wine from the neighboring region of Liguria such as Vermentino.

 YIELDS 1 FLATBREAD

INGREDIENTS

5 oz (142 g) oiled Pizza Dough ball (page 17)

Extra virgin olive oil

5–6 very thinly sliced pieces of Prosciutto di Parma

3-oz (85 g) wedge of Parmigiano Reggiano

DIRECTIONS

Lightly grease a metal work surface and the palms of your hands. Place the dough ball in the center of the surface and press down evenly with the palm of your hand. Working with both hands, start in the middle and spread the dough out with your palms while stretching the outer edges with your fingers. You should have an approximately 12 by 8 inch (30 x 20 cm) rectangle.

Lift up the edge farthest from yourself and slide your fingers under the dough. Move to the direct zone of your grill and place the bottom edge of the dough at the farthest point from you and pull the dough toward you to place on grill. Gently lift up 1 edge of the dough with the tongs to check for color. When you see some color setting in, lift the dough and give it a quarter turn with the peel. When the dough is sufficiently browned on the bottom, but not charred, remove it from the direct zone and flip it over onto the indirect zone.

Drizzle with a modest amount of olive oil (perhaps 1 to 2 tablespoons [15 to 30 ml] maximum) and brush the crust. Move to the direct side of the grill and rotate every 15 to 30 seconds until the bottom is crispy. When the bottom is crispy, move to the indirect side of the grill. Working quickly, remove the flatbread from the grill and arrange the prosciutto nicely around the flatbread, shave the Parmigiano Reggiano all over the flatbread, drizzle with the olive oil, slice and serve.

AGLIO, OLIO AND PEPPERONCINO GRILLED FLATBREAD

This flatbread is about as simple as it gets and is great served alongside cured meats and cheeses. Keep in mind all chiles have a different heat level. Take a bite of one of the slices to determine how much of it you want to use. Try it with a well-chilled Trebbiano.

 YIELDS 1 FLATBREAD

INGREDIENTS

2 tbsp (30 ml) extra virgin olive oil

2 cloves of garlic, thinly sliced

5 oz (142 g) oiled Pizza Dough ball (page 17)

1 small serrano chile pepper (you can substitute jalapeño if needed), sliced thinly

Flaky sea salt (such as Maldon), for garnish

DIRECTIONS

Heat the oil in a small skillet over medium heat. Add the garlic and cook until translucent. Pour the oil and garlic into a small bowl and reserve.

Lightly grease a metal work surface and the palms of your hands. Place the dough ball in the center of the surface and press down evenly with the palm of your hand. Working with both hands, start in the middle and spread the dough out with your palms while stretching the outer edges with your fingers. You should have an approximately 12 by 8 inch (30 x 20 cm) rectangle.

Lift up the edge farthest from yourself and slide your fingers under the dough. Move to the direct zone of your grill and place the bottom edge of the dough at the farthest point from you and pull the dough toward you to place on grill. Gently lift up 1 edge of the dough with the tongs to check for color. When you see some color setting in, lift the dough and give it a quarter turn with the peel. When the dough is sufficiently browned on the bottom, but not charred, remove it from the direct zone and flip it over onto the indirect zone.

Drizzle with half of the garlic-infused olive oil and brush the crust. Spoon the remaining oil and garlic mixture all around the flatbread and sprinkle as many of the chiles as you want around the flatbread. Move to the direct side of the grill and rotate every 15 to 30 seconds until the bottom is crispy. Remove from the grill, sprinkle with the flaky salt, slice and serve.

GOAT CHEESE, TOMATO AND OLIVE FLATBREAD

This is another flatbread that should be made at the height of tomato season. The tartness of the goat cheese is perfectly offset by the briny olives. Try to use the freshest local goat cheese you can find; the difference in flavor is well worth searching for it.

 YIELDS 1 FLATBREAD

INGREDIENTS

5 oz (142 g) oiled Pizza Dough ball (page 17)

Extra virgin olive oil

3 oz (85 g) fresh goat cheese

1 medium ripe tomato, sliced into ⅛-inch (3 mm) slices

¼ c (35 g) chopped Moroccan oil-cured olives

Thinly sliced scallions (green part only)

Freshly ground black pepper

DIRECTIONS

Lightly grease a metal work surface and the palms of your hands. Place the dough ball in the center of the surface and press down evenly with the palm of your hand. Working with both hands, start in the middle and spread the dough out with your palms while stretching the outer edges with your fingers. You should have an approximately 12 by 8 inch (30 x 20 cm) rectangle.

Lift up the edge farthest from yourself and slide your fingers under the dough. Move to the direct zone of your grill and place the bottom edge of the dough at the farthest point from you and pull the dough toward you to place on grill. Gently lift up 1 edge of the dough with the tongs to check for color. When you see some color setting in, lift the dough and give it a quarter turn with the peel. When the dough is sufficiently browned on the bottom, but not charred, remove it from the direct zone and flip it over onto the indirect zone.

Drizzle with olive oil and brush the crust evenly. Spread the cheese all over the pizza crust using the back of a spoon. Place the tomatoes all around and scatter the chopped olives. Move the flatbread to the direct side of the grill and rotate every 15 to 30 seconds until the bottom is crispy. Remove the flatbread, sprinkle the scallions and freshly ground black pepper. Drizzle some more olive oil around the flatbread, slice and serve.

CARTA MUSICA FLATBREAD

This is a very simple flatbread using just a little bit of cheese, oil and herbs. It is great in a breadbasket and goes well with salads, dips and spreads. If you can manage to crisp up the top of the pizza without turning it a quarter turn, the pizza will look like a sheet of music, hence the name.

 YIELDS I FLATBREAD

INGREDIENTS

5 oz (142 g) oiled Pizza Dough ball (page 17)

Extra virgin olive oil

¼ c (35 g) grated Parmesan

¼ c (35 g) grated Romano

Pinch of thinly slice flat-leaf parsley

Fresh thyme leaves or rosemary, picked from the stem not chopped

Kosher salt or large grain/flaky sea salt (such as Maldon)

Black pepper (optional)

DIRECTIONS

Lightly grease a metal work surface and the palms of your hands. Place the dough ball in the center of the surface and press down evenly with the palm of your hand. Working with both hands, start in the middle and spread the dough out with your palms while stretching the outer edges with your fingers. You should have an approximately 12 by 8 inch (30 x 20 cm) rectangle.

Lift up the edge farthest from yourself and slide your fingers under the dough. Move to the direct zone of your grill and place the bottom edge of the dough at the farthest point from you and pull the dough toward you to place on grill. Gently lift up 1 edge of the dough with the tongs to check for color. Try to crisp the top without turning it a quarter turn. When the dough is sufficiently browned on the bottom, but not charred, remove it from the direct zone and flip it over onto the indirect zone.

Drizzle with olive oil and brush the crust. Sprinkle on the Parmesan, Romano and herbs and move the pizza to the direct side of the grill and crisp to desired doneness. Remove the flatbread from the grill and drizzle some olive oil around and sprinkle a little bit of sea salt. Crack some black pepper over the top if you wish. Bring to the table whole and break bread with your friends. If you make 3 or 4 of them and bring them all to the table it will look like you are bringing a book of music to be shared, except of course it is bread to be eaten—even better.

ITALIAN TUNA SALAD ON GRILLED ROMANO FLATBREAD

This is my favorite tuna salad but instead of serving it with or over lettuce I prefer to put it on a flatbread. I really enjoy this for lunch on a sunny day sitting in the backyard sipping on a nice cold Falanghina. This flatbread is best eaten with a knife and fork.

 **YIELDS | FLATBREAD**

INGREDIENTS

7 oz (198 g) tuna packed in oil (1 can)

1 rib of celery, sliced very thinly crosswise

½ very small red onion, sliced thinly across the grain

¼ c (35 g) unstuffed green olives, cut into quarters

2 tbsp (17 g) capers, rinsed

8 large basil leaves, torn into pieces

1 sprig parsley, leaves removed and sliced

¼ c (60 ml) extra virgin olive oil, plus more for the flatbread

¼ c (60 ml) red wine vinegar

Salt

Pepper

10 small grape or cherry tomatoes, cut in half

5 oz (142 g) oiled Pizza Dough ball (page 17)

¾ c (105 g) grated Romano cheese

DIRECTIONS

Prepare the salad. Combine the tuna, celery, red onion, olives, capers, basil, parsley, ¼ cup (60 ml) of olive oil and the red wine vinegar in a bowl. Season to taste with salt and pepper. The salad can be made and refrigerated up to 4 hours before making the flatbread. When it is time to prepare the flatbread add the tomatoes to the salad, toss to combine and recheck the seasoning.

Lightly grease a metal work surface and the palms of your hands. Place the dough ball in the center of the surface and press down evenly with the palm of your hand. Working with both hands, start in the middle and spread the dough out with your palms while stretching the outer edges with your fingers. You should have an approximately 12 by 8 inch (30 x 20 cm) rectangle.

Lift up the edge farthest from yourself and slide your fingers under the dough. Move to the direct zone of your grill and place the bottom edge of the dough at the farthest point from you and pull the dough toward you to place on grill. Gently lift up 1 edge of the dough with the tongs to check for color. When you see some color setting in, lift the dough and give it a quarter turn with the peel. When the dough is sufficiently browned on the bottom, but not charred, remove it from the direct zone and flip it over onto the indirect zone.

When you turn the flatbread over onto the indirect side of the grill, brush it with olive oil and sprinkle ½ cup (70 g) of the Romano cheese all across the top. Move the flatbread to the direct side of the grill and rotate the pizza every 15 to 30 seconds until the bottom is crispy. Remove the flatbread to a plate, arrange the salad around the flatbread and sprinkle the remaining ¼ cup (35 g) of Romano. Serve.

EGGPLANT CAVIAR AND OLIVE FLATBREAD

Eggplant caviar is a versatile condiment that can be used as a spread or dip or a side dish for grilled meats. I use it here on a Middle Eastern–inspired flatbread.

➡ YIELDS 1 FLATBREAD

INGREDIENTS

5 oz (142 g) oiled Pizza Dough ball (page 17)

Extra virgin olive oil

1 c (140 g) Pizza Cheese Blend (page 20)

1 c (160 g) Eggplant Caviar (page 195)

¼ c (35 g) chopped cured Moroccan olives

1 tbsp (3 g) thinly sliced flat-leaf parsley, for garnish

DIRECTIONS

Lightly grease a metal work surface and the palms of your hands. Place the dough ball in the center of the surface and press down evenly with the palm of your hand. Working with both hands, start in the middle and spread the dough out with your palms while stretching the outer edges with your fingers. You should have an approximately 12 by 8 inch (30 x 20 cm) rectangle.

Lift up the edge farthest from yourself and slide your fingers under the dough. Move to the direct zone of your grill and place the bottom edge of the dough at the farthest point from you and pull the dough toward you to place on grill. Gently lift up 1 edge of the dough with the tongs to check for color. When you see some color setting in, lift the dough and give it a quarter turn with the peel. When the dough is sufficiently browned on the bottom, but not charred, remove it from the direct zone and flip it over onto the indirect zone.

Drizzle with olive oil and brush the crust evenly. Sprinkle on the pizza cheese and scatter tablespoon-size dollops of the eggplant caviar all around the flatbread. Sprinkle the chopped olives evenly and then move the flatbread to the direct side of the grill and rotate every 15 to 30 seconds to evenly crisp the bottom. Remove from the grill, sprinkle with the sliced parsley and drizzle a little more olive oil around the flatbread. Slice and serve.

EGGPLANT CAVIAR

➤ YIELDS 2 CUPS (320 G)

INGREDIENTS

2 lb (900 g) eggplant, cut in half lengthwise (2 medium)

1 shallot, minced

4 cloves of garlic, minced

2 tbsp (30 ml) olive oil

1 c (240 ml) diced canned tomatoes, drained of their juices

1 tbsp (15 ml) lemon juice

Salt

Freshly ground black pepper

DIRECTIONS

Preheat the oven to 350°F (177°C).

Place the eggplant on a cookie sheet, cut-side up, and roast for approximately 30 minutes or until soft.

Remove from the oven and cool. When the eggplant is cool, scoop out the flesh and place in the bowl of a food processor and process until smooth. Place the eggplant in a bowl. Sauté the shallots and garlic in the olive oil until soft and slightly translucent. Stir into the eggplant, add the tomatoes and lemon juice and season to taste with the salt and pepper.

WICKED GOOD BARBECUE DEEP-DISH PIZZA

The only pan pizza in the book—just because. I wanted to give people an opportunity to use their grill as a true oven and a smoker for at least one pizza. I turned to my friend and barbecue teammate Chris Hart for advice. This is what he sent me. Check out Chris and Andy Husbands' *Wicked Good Barbecue* for more suggestions. The barbeque pork fatty requires one day of advance preparation.

➜ YIELDS I (12" [30.5 CM]) PIZZA

INGREDIENTS

2 lb (900 g) Smoked Barbecue Pork Fatty (page 197)

10 oz (285 g) oiled Pizza Dough ball (page 17)

1 c (240 ml) barbecue sauce

1 c (140 g) shredded whole-milk Mozzarella

2 tbsp (25 g) barbecue dry rub

2 tbsp (30 ml) extra virgin olive oil

DIRECTIONS

Remove fatty from the refrigerator and cut into ⅛ inch (3 mm) slices. Set aside on a platter to come to room temperature.

Prepare a grill for 2 zone grilling. When the temperature inside the grill is at 425°F (218°C), it is ready.

Brush olive oil on the inside of a 12-inch (30 cm) cast-iron pan. Spread the dough into the pan. The dough should be about ½-inch (13 mm) thick on the bottom and extend about 1 inch (2.5 cm) up the sides. Sprinkle the dough with the barbecue dry rub. Poke some holes in the dough with the tines of a fork. Place the cast-iron pan on the indirect zone of the grill and close the lid. Cook for 7 minutes. Open the lid, rotate pan 180 degrees, close the lid and cook an additional 5 minutes. With oven mitts remove the pan from the grill and place on a trivet.

Spoon ½ cup (120 ml) of the barbecue sauce evenly into the bottom of the pizza. Layer half of the fatty slices on top of the sauce, sprinkle the cheese evenly onto the pizza. Drizzle ¼ cup (60 ml) of the sauce over the pizza and add the remaining slices of the fatty. Drizzle the remaining sauce over the sausage. Return to the grill on the indirect side, close the lid and cook for 5 minutes. Rotate the pan 180 degrees, close the lid and cook an additional 5 minutes or until the sauce and cheese are bubbling. Remove from the grill and place on a trivet, let the pizza rest for 5 minutes, slice and serve.

SMOKED BARBECUE PORK FATTY

In barbecue cooking circles, a fatty is a large rolled tube of sausage that is smoked. There are many different versions of stuffed and wrapped fatties too. This is the simplest version.

➡ YIELDS 2 POUNDS (900 G)

INGREDIENTS

2 lb (900 g) sweet Italian pork sausage, removed from casings

2 tbsp (25 g) barbecue dry rub

DIRECTIONS

Form sausage into a log about 4 inches (10 cm) in diameter, sprinkle the exterior with the barbecue dry rub.

Prepare a smoker at 250°F (121°C).

Smoke the sausage until the internal temperature in the middle reaches 150°F (66°C), about 1½ hours.

Remove the sausage from the smoker, let rest for 30 minutes and refrigerate overnight.

GARLIC SPINACH WITH WARM BACON VINAIGRETTE AND SHAVED ROMANO FLATBREAD

This is another version of a salad served on a flatbread. Wilting the spinach with the garlic intensifies the flavor of the spinach and the bacon brings out a nice smoky contrast.

 YIELDS | FLATBREAD

INGREDIENTS

2 tbsp (30 ml) olive oil

2 cloves of garlic, minced

10 oz (284 g) leafy green spinach, stems removed

Salt

Freshly ground black pepper

2 tbsp (30 ml) reserved bacon fat

2 tbsp (30 ml) red wine vinegar

5 oz (142 g) oiled Pizza Dough ball (page 17)

Extra virgin olive oil

½ c (70 g) Pizza Cheese Blend (page 20)

3 slices smoked bacon, cut into 1-inch (2.5 cm) pieces, cooked to crispy (reserve fat)

½ of a very small red onion, sliced thinly crosswise

3-oz (85 g) wedge of Pecorino Romano (it is hard to make shavings from anything smaller)

DIRECTIONS

In a sauté pan, heat the olive oil and add the garlic and cook until it is translucent. Add the spinach, season with salt and pepper and cook just until wilted, remove from the pan and place in a colander to let the juices drain.

Make the vinaigrette. Combine the bacon fat and red wine vinegar in a small saucepan, season with salt and pepper to taste and place in a warm spot near or on the grill to keep the bacon fat melted.

Lightly grease a metal work surface and the palms of your hands. Place the dough ball in the center of the surface and press down evenly with the palm of your hand. Working with both hands, start in the middle and spread the dough out with your palms while stretching the outer edges with your fingers. You should have an approximately 12 by 8 inch (30 x 20 cm) rectangle.

Lift up the edge farthest from yourself and slide your fingers under the dough. Move to the direct zone of your grill and place the bottom edge of the dough at the farthest point from you and pull the dough toward you to place on grill. Gently lift up 1 edge of the dough with the tongs to check for color. When you see some color setting in, lift the dough and give it a quarter turn with the peel. When the dough is sufficiently browned on the bottom, but not charred, remove it from the direct zone and flip it over onto the indirect zone.

Drizzle lightly with olive oil and brush the crust evenly. Sprinkle the cheese evenly across the crust, add the spinach and bacon and close the lid for about 30 seconds to a minute to just heat up the spinach and bacon. Move the flatbread to the direct side of the grill and rotate every 15 to 30 seconds until the bottom is crispy. Move the flatbread to the indirect side of the grill, add the onions, stir the vinaigrette and drizzle it all around. Using a vegetable peeler, shave thin slices of the Romano all around the flatbread. As much as you like. Remove, slice and serve.

ABOUT THE AUTHOR

JOHN DELPHA is a former Army officer and helicopter pilot turned chef. His first professional cooking job was at the acclaimed Al Forno in Providence, RI, where he learned how to grill pizza the right way. He has cooked in and directed some of the best kitchens in Boston such as Clio, Mistral, Harvest, Sorellina and La Campania. He has a passion for live-fire cooking and is a member of the 2009 Jack Daniel's World Barbecue Championship cooking team iQue. He has won the "I Know Jack About Grillin'" contest twice and has taken home the top honor in the Cook's Choice category at "the Jack" on two occasions, as well as two separate perfect scores in the dessert category. When he isn't running a commercial kitchen he prefers to be outdoors, hiking, biking, cooking barbecue and grilling at competitions.

ACKNOWLEDGMENTS

I would like to thank ...

My parents, for all the sacrifices they made to give my sister and me a proper upbringing.

Dad, for being pissed off when he found out I went to Airborne school via a local newspaper.

Mom, for going with the flow, for all the lunches at Twin Oaks for good report cards and the deliveries from Mr. D's Deli in grammar school.

My sister, for only throwing Tabasco sauce in my eyes once and for her amazing baked stuffed shrimp.

My barbecue teammates, Chris Hart, Andy Husbands, Jamie Hart, Ken Goodman, Ed Doyle and Dave Frary for inviting me into the world of competition barbecue.

Chris Hart, for allowing me to cook the stuff I wanted to cook for the big contests.

Andy and Chris, for the two-time win in the " I Know Jack About Grillin'" contest at "the Jack."

Ken Goodman, for bringing this book to life in a way I never would have expected. You rock, my brother.

Will Kiester, for giving me this opportunity.

Marissa Giambelluca, for the unwavering patience and for putting up with a first-time author.

My brothers and sisters in the U.S. Army, I'd come back in a heartbeat.

My fellow aviators in the Rhode Island Army National Guard, especially the more experienced guys that taught us all "the right way" to do things.

Johanne Killeen and George Germon, for hiring me and having faith in someone with no real experience.

Ken Oringer, for the opportunity to cook on multiple continents and for our culinary think sessions.

Chip Henderson, for covering my six. "I don't believe I'd a told that..."

My support group, Jack Daniel's, Jim Beam, George Dickel, Pappy Van Winkle, Joe Cassinelli, Sal Fristensky et al.

My wife Katy, for the great late-night meals, unwavering support and other stuff. ☺

Ginger and Lucky, for being the best dog friends ever.

You, for buying this book and having fun with it.

INDEX